DIGGING UP THE PAST

GENESIS 3-11

KAY ARTHUR
JANNA ARNDT

HARVEST HOUSE PUBLISHERS
Eugene, Oregon 97402

Scripture quotations in this book are taken from the New American Standard Bible ®, © 1960, 1962, 1963, 1968, 1971, 1972, 1973, 1975, 1977, 1995 by The Lockman Foundation. Used by permission.

DISCOVER 4 YOURSELF is a registered trademark of The Hawkins Children's LLC. Harvest House Publishers is the exclusive licensee of the federally registered trademark DISCOVER 4 YOURSELF.

Illustrations by Steve Bjorkman

Cover by Left Coast Design, Portland, Oregon

Discover 4 Yourself® Inductive Bible Studies for Kids
DIGGING UP THE PAST

Published by Harvest House Publishers
Eugene, Oregon 97402
www.harvesthousepublishers.com

ISBN-13: 978-0-7369-0374-5
ISBN-10: 0-7369-0374-7

Printed in the United States of America.

06 07 08 09 10 11 12 / ML-MS / 12 11 10 9 8 7 6 5 4 3

For my nieces and nephew
Mary Frances, Hannah, and David Usry.
May you find favor with God just like Noah, who lived in a world full of wickedness yet he was found to be a righteous man, blameless in his time. He walked with God.
I love you.
Aunt Janna
Philippians 4:8

CONTENTS

Digging for Truth:
A Bible Study *You* Can Do!

DIGGING FOR TRUTH: A BIBLE STUDY YOU CAN DO!

Look, Molly, here they come! Do you see them?" asked Max as he watched the Jeep bumping along the road, racing toward the camp.

You're back! And, like Max and Molly, we're so happy you have joined us for our new adventure in Genesis Part Two. We are going to have so much fun as we continue to help Uncle Jake on his archaeological dig. Who knows what we will discover next? There are so many neat things to uncover as we continue to study the Book of Genesis.

We need to find out what happens after God creates a perfect world. Is the world still a perfect place today? What happened in the Garden of Eden? Why did Adam and Eve leave? What major catastrophe happened to the earth, and why did it happen? How did man get scattered all over the earth, and why do people in different countries speak different languages? Looks like we have a lot of exciting things to uncover, doesn't it?

You can find all the answers by studying God's Word, the Bible, and by asking God's Spirit to lead and guide you. You also have this book, which is an inductive Bible study. That word *inductive* means this study will help you investigate the Book of Genesis and discover *for yourself* what it means, instead of depending on what someone else says it means. It's just like what you did in Genesis Part One.

So are you ready to dig up the truth? Great! Then check out the supply list and make sure you have everything you need for our big adventure in Genesis Part Two.

Race you to the tent!

New American Standard Bible (Updated Edition—or preferably the *New Inductive Study Bible*, the NISB)
Pen or Pencil
Colored Pencils
Index Cards
A Dictionary
This Workbook

1

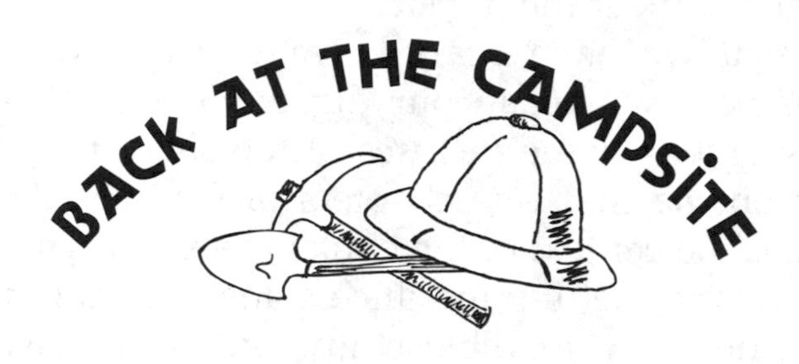

GENESIS 1–11

Whew, what a race! We could sure use an ice-cold lemonade. How about you? Let's hurry and unpack your gear, then we can get something to drink on our way to the main campsite. We need to meet Uncle Jake and the dig team for a very important meeting so we can get started digging up more truths in Genesis.

MEETING WITH THE TEAM

"Hey, guys, I see you're ready to get started," said Uncle Jake as we walked up to the main campsite. "Let's start by talking with our 'site boss.' "

Do you remember WHO our "site boss" is? That's right—it's God! Remember, we can't do anything without God's help. We need His Holy Spirit to lead and guide us into all truth so that we will understand the things we discover in His Word and how He wants us to apply those truths to our lives. So before we do anything else, we need to go to God in prayer. Then we need to remember to pray first thing every day before we start our work at the dig site.

Now that we have prayed, we're ready to go. Do you remember how we began our dig in Genesis Part One? We started by getting some pictures of the site through doing an overview on the first five chapters of Genesis. An overview helps us see the context of the book we are studying.

Context is the setting in which something is found. This is important not only in Bible study, but in archaeology also. Context is a combination of two words: *con* which means "with," and *text* which means "what is written." So when you look for context in the Bible, you look at the verses and chapters surrounding the passage you are studying.

Context also includes:

- The place where something happens. (This is geographical context, like the Fertile Crescent and not the United States and Canada.)

- The time in history an event happens. (This is historical context, such as the time before Noah and the flood or the time after the flood.)

- The customs of a group of people. (This is cultural context. For instance, in Bible times people lived in tents like Abraham. Abraham was a very rich man who lived in tents instead of in a house. Also, they wore tunics and not blue jeans or khakis.)

We discover context by observation. We begin by looking at the things that are obvious (those are the things that are the easiest to see). In the Bible the three easiest things to see are always:

1. people (WHO?)

2. places (WHERE?)

3. events (WHAT?)

Let's get started on our overview. Ben, our site artist, is going to help us uncover the main event in Genesis 3. The first thing we need to do is look at our Observation Worksheets. We need to read Genesis 3, on page 192, and look for what is most obvious, the easiest thing to see. Ask yourself: WHAT is happening in this chapter? Then write a title for the main event on the line under the box below. A title is a very brief description that tells what the main event is. A title should:

1. be as short as possible
2. describe the main thing the chapter is about
3. if possible, use words you find in the chapter instead of your own words
4. be easy to remember
5. be different from the other titles so that you can tell them apart

Then after you have read the chapter and discovered the main event of Genesis 3, draw it on our sketch pad in the box below.

Genesis 3

The Tree of forbidden fruit

All right! Now before we head to the mess tent, let's review a skill we learned in Genesis Part One that could be very important on our dig. Let's practice our hieroglyphic decoding skills by uncovering our memory verse. Find the word that matches the drawing by looking at our hieroglyphic code box. Then write the word that matches the picture on the blanks underneath the symbols.

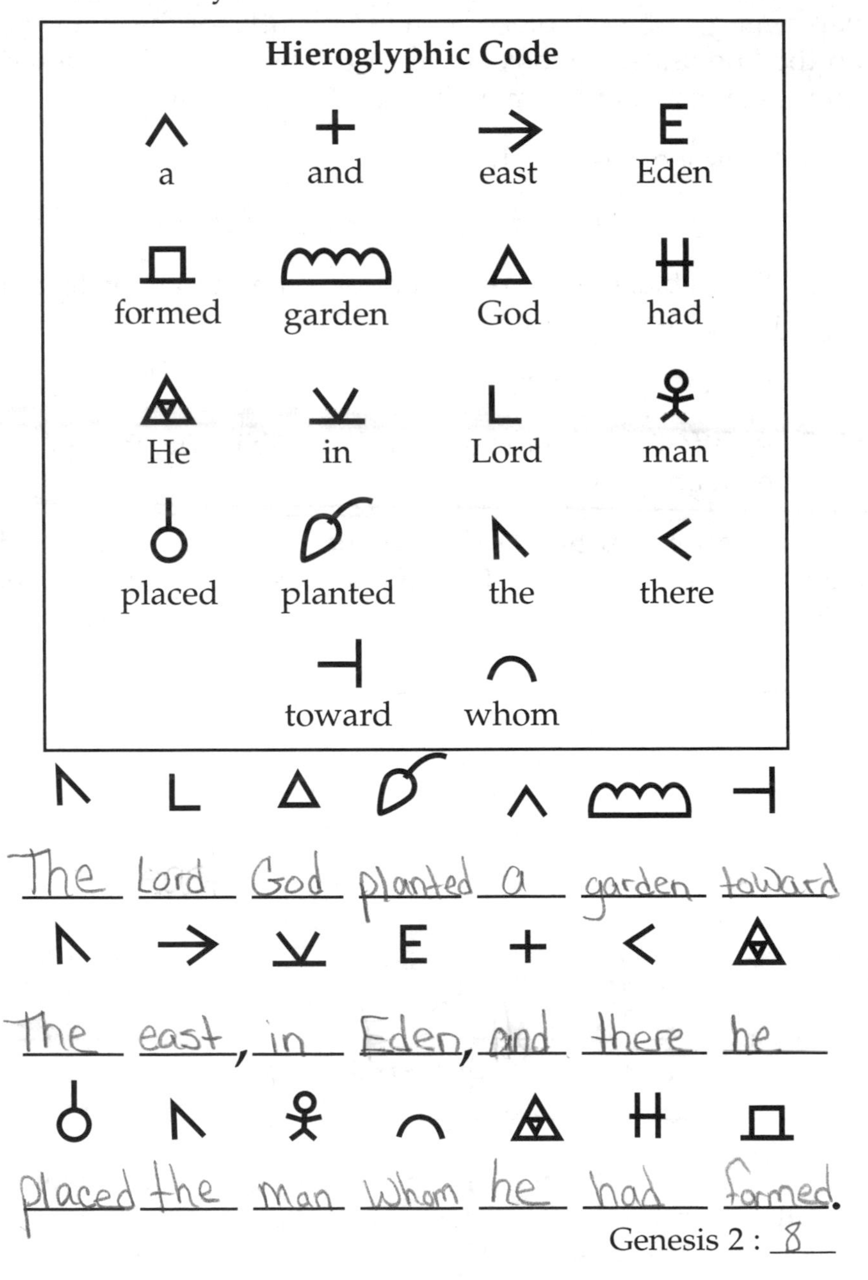

Now write your memory verse on an index card and practice saying it aloud three times in a row, three times today. Way to go!

Day Two

SKETCHING THE MAIN EVENTS

Hey, wake up, sleepyhead! It's time for breakfast, and we have a lot to discover today. Ben, our site artist, wants us to head over to his tent as soon as we finish eating so we can uncover the main events in Genesis 4 and 5.

"Come on in, guys," Ben called out as we approached the opening of his tent. "I was just gathering up our sketch pads and pencils so we can take our gear and go sit by the stream while we do our research today."

"That's a great idea," Max said. Ben handed Max and Molly their sketch pads as they walked to the stream and sat next to the water.

"Okay, Max," questioned Ben, "tell me: What should we do first?"

"Pray!" said Max.

"Good! Why don't you lead us in prayer, Max, and then we will be ready to head to Genesis 4."

Okay, junior archaeologists, turn to page 195 and read Genesis 4. Then sketch the main event in the box below and put the title for the event on the line under the box.

Genesis 4

Cain murdered Abel

Very artistic! Now let's do it one more time for Genesis 5. Read Genesis 5, then sketch the main event in the box below and give it a title.

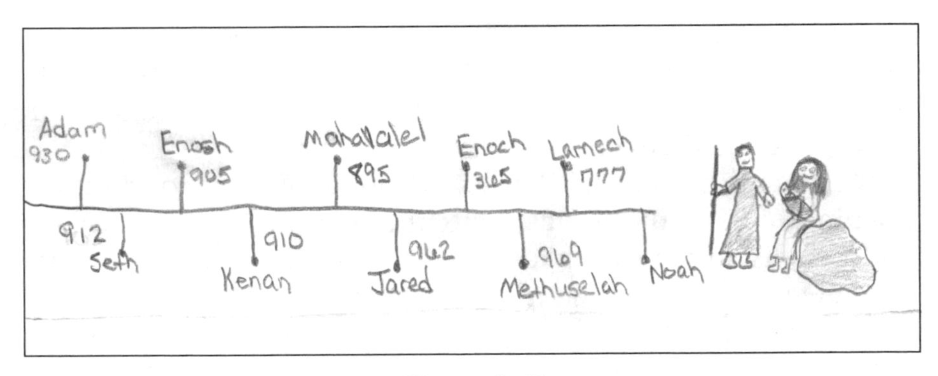

Genesis 5

Generation Were Born

Awesome! Now practice saying your memory verse three times today.

MORE SKETCHES

"I like working on these sketches, Max. Maybe I'll be a site artist like Ben when I finish school."

"That would be really cool, Molly. Your drawings are really good!"

"Thanks, Max. We better hurry. Ben will be waiting for us at the stream, and I can't wait to get started on Genesis 6."

"Okay, Molly. Let me find Sam's leash. Uh-oh, where's Sam?"

"Oh no, Max! Don't tell me he's loose. There's no telling what he'll be into next."

"Why don't you head to the stream, Molly, and tell Ben I'll be there in a few minutes. I'll go check out the mess tent. Sam's probably begging Mr. Jim for some bacon. You know how Sam loves bacon!"

"Okay, Max. See you in a little while."

"Hi, Ben," Molly called out.

"Hi, Molly. Where are Max and Sam?"

"Sam's loose again. Max will catch up as soon as he tracks down Sam."

"Okay, Molly. Let's spend some time with our 'site boss,' and then we can get started on Genesis 6."

Turn to page 201 of your Observation Worksheets and read Genesis 6. After you finish reading, draw the main event in the box. Make up a title and place it on the line underneath.

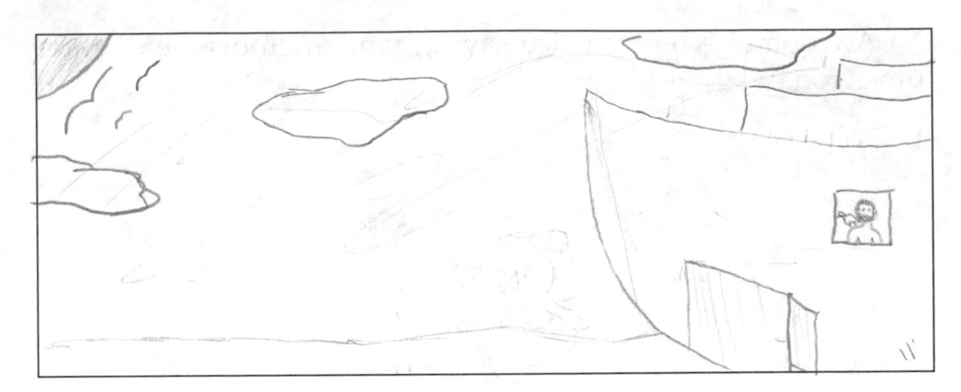

Genesis 6

"Noah & the animals adventure"

Now let's do the same thing by reading Genesis 7 and sketching it out in the box below. Then add a title.

Genesis 7

"Forty Day & Nights"

Magnificent! Uh-oh, clear a path. Here come Max and Sam. "Hold tight, Max," yelled Molly. "Watch out! He's headed for the stream." SPLASH! Molly's warning came at the moment Sam yanked free and landed in the water.

"Quit laughing, Molly. You, too, Ben! Help me get this crazy dog out of the water. Sam, you are in big-time trouble!"

Why don't you help Max, Molly, and Ben coax Sam out of the water, and we'll see you back at the campsite. Don't forget to practice your memory verse!

BACK TO THE DRAWING BOARD

"Quit laughing, Molly! It wasn't that funny."

"But it was, Max. You should have seen yourself holding on to Sam's leash with all your might and Sam flying across the ground at a breakneck pace. It was hilarious. I just can't get it out of my mind."

"How would you like being on the other end of that leash? I'll let you take Sam on his next trip to the stream."

"No way, Max. Remember, he's your dog."

"Okay, guys," laughed Ben. "We better get to work. We only have four more sketches to go."

What's next, junior archaeologists? What is the first thing we need to do? P _r_ _a_ y. Good for you. You've got it down.

Turn to your Observation Worksheets and read Genesis 8.

Sketch the main event in Genesis 8 below and then add a title.

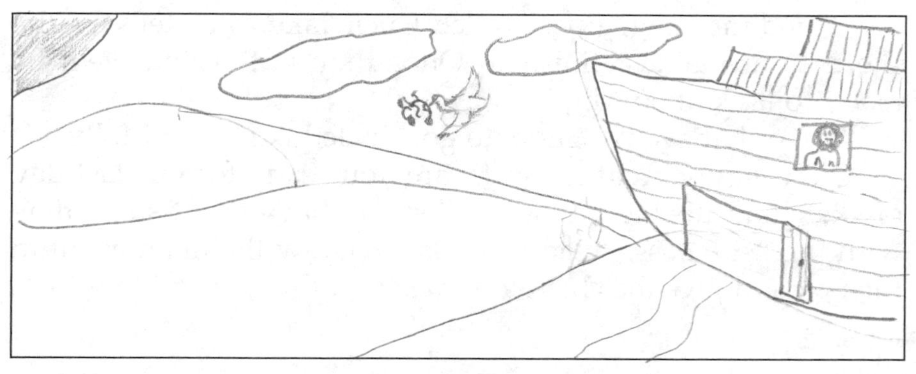

Genesis 8

The Olive branch

Now read Genesis 9 and sketch out the main event and write a title.

Genesis 9

Colors of Promise

Terrific! Hang in there—only two more sketches and we will be ready to dig!

THE FINAL SKETCHES

"Good morning, guys," called Uncle Jake. "Ben tells me the sketches are almost finished. Once they're finished we'll be ready to lay out our dig."

"We only have two more to go, Uncle Jake," said Molly.

Okay, junior archaeologists, are you ready for our last day of sketching the big picture? After you have spent some time with the "site boss," read Genesis 10. Draw the main event in the box and give the chapter a title.

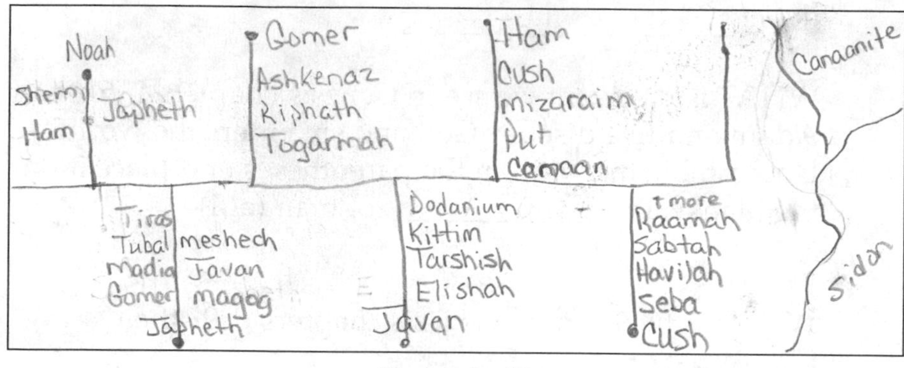

Genesis 10

Many Sons

Now one more chapter and our sketches will be complete. Read Genesis 11. Draw your last sketch and give it a title.

Genesis 11

Langugues

Excellent work! Uncle Jake is impressed! Maybe you will want to be a site artist one day.

Now before we head to the campfire, we need to look at all we have discovered this week.

Let's review Genesis chapters 1–11. Did you know we can divide these 11 chapters up to show four different events that are very important? Let's see if we can figure out WHAT those four events are by looking back at our sketches.

WHAT is the main event in Genesis chapters 1 and 2? (We did this in Genesis Part One.)

the C r e a t i o n

WHAT is the event we see in Genesis chapters 3–5 when Adam and Eve disobey God and sin enters the world? Unscramble the word in the parentheses and place it on the blanks. the f a l l of man (alfl)

WHAT is the event in Genesis chapters 6–9? the f l o o d

WHAT is the event in Genesis chapters 10–11? Unscramble the word in parentheses and place it on the blanks. the n a t i o n s (atnoins)

Isn't that awesome? You have uncovered the four major events that take place in Genesis 1–11. This is a great way to remember what happens in the first part of the Book of Genesis.

Now here are a few motions to help you remember these four events. Take your hand and place it under your chin and speak. This represents Creation because God said it, and it was created.

Now act like you are about to stumble as you walk. This represents the fall of man.

Third, take your hands and pretend the waters are rising. Move your hands up slowly and raise them over your head saying, "Blub, blub, blub." This represents the flood.

And for the last part of Genesis 1–11, take your left hand and place it out to the side, palm up, and say, "Shem." Do the same thing with your right hand and say, "Ham." Nod your head forward and say, "Japheth." These are the nations.

Now practice this until you can say all four of these events from memory:

Genesis 1–2 Creation,

Genesis 3–5 The Fall,

Genesis 6–9 The Flood,

and Genesis 10–11 The Nations.

Then show it to a friend or a grown-up. And don't forget to say your memory verse to someone this week, too.

2

GENESIS 3

Now that our sketches are finished and we have the big picture of what happens in Genesis 1–11, it's time for us to head back to the pit. Grab your shovels, picks, and brushes along with a hat to shield your face from the sun, and we'll meet you at the pit.

EXCAVATING A SQUARE

"Okay, guys, let's look at the top plan that Ben, Max, and Molly have drawn for us," Uncle Jake called out as the dig team gathered around the pit. "William will divide you into groups of twos and threes, and then he will assign each group a square to excavate."

Now before we get started, let's look over our research. We know from doing Genesis Part One that Genesis 1 is about God creating the world and all that is in it. Genesis 2 gives us more details concerning the sixth day of Creation when God created man.

As William hands out our assignments, we need to dig up the evidence in Genesis 3 that tells us if the perfect world God created in Genesis 1 and 2 stayed a perfect place and, if it didn't, what happened to change it.

"Is everyone ready?" asked Uncle Jake. "Good. Let's begin by praying. William, will you lead the team in prayer?"

Okay, junior archaeologists, we are ready to begin. You have been assigned to excavate square B3, so grab your *patish* (that's your hand pick). Use it to loosen the soil. Let's get started by digging up our key words.

What are key words? Key words are words that pop up more than once. They are called key words because they help unlock the meaning of the chapter or book that you are studying and give you clues about what is most important in a passage of Scripture. Do you remember doing this in *How to Study Your Bible for Kids*?

- Key words are usually used over and over again.
- Key words are important.
- Key words are used by the writer for a reason.

Once you discover a key word, you need to mark it in a special way using a special color or symbol so that you can immediately spot it in Scripture. You also need to watch and see if there are any pronouns or synonyms that go with the key word and mark them also. What are pronouns and synonyms? Take a look at your maps.

PRONOUN MAP

Pronouns are words that take the place of nouns. A noun is a person, place, or thing. A pronoun stands in for a noun. Here's an example: "Molly and Max race to the dig site. They can't wait to get started." The word they is a pronoun because it takes the place of Molly's and Max's names in the second sentence. It is another word we use to refer to Molly and Max.

Watch for these other pronouns when you are marking words referring to people:

I	you	he	she
me	yours	him	her
mine		his	hers
we	it		
our	its		
they	them		

SYNONYM MAP

Synonyms are different words that mean the same thing.

For example, *sailboat, yacht,* and *rowboat* are different words, but they are all names of boats. That's a synonym.

Now that you know what key words, pronouns, and synonyms are, turn to page 189 of your Observation Worksheets on Genesis. Read all of Genesis 2 to put you in context. After you have read Genesis 2, read Genesis 3, and then mark the following key words from Genesis 2:15–3:24. Also mark anything that tells you WHEN something happened with a green clock like this:

God (Lord God) (draw a purple triangle and color it yellow—don't forget to watch for pronouns)

man (Adam)(color it orange)

woman (Eve, wife)(color it pink)

die (draw a black tombstone and color it brown)

serpent (red pitchfork)

eat (circle in blue)

tree of the knowledge of good and evil (draw a tree and put some red fruit on the tree)

cursed (draw a box in orange and color it brown)

That was some great digging! Before you head to the showers to cool off and wash away all that dirt and grime, we need for you to excavate the squares that we have marked out on our grid to find your memory verse. Use the letter/number pair under each blank. Go to the grid and find the letter, such as A on the right side of the grid, and then go up until you find the number that goes with the A, such as 4. Find the letter in the square that goes with A4 and write it on the blank. Do the same thing for each blank until you have discovered your verse for the week. We've done the first one for you.

T H E

C4 C3 A5 A3 D1 B2 D5 A1 D1 D5

C2 D1 B1 B1 B3 E2 D5 A5 D5 C4 C3 A5 B1 B3 E2

E5 B3 A2 B4 E2 A1, “D2 B2 D1 B1 B3 E2 A2

C4 B2 A5 A5 D1 D2 C4 C3 A5 A1 B3 B2 D5 A5 E2

A2 D1 E3 B1 B3 A2 A5 B3 C4 D2 B2 A5 A5 A3 A2;

D4 E3 C4 D2 B2 D1 B1 C4 C3 A5 C4 B2 A5 A5

D1 D2 C4 C3 A5 C5 E2 D1 D3 A3 A5 D5 A1 A5 D1 D2

A1 D1 D1 D5 B3 E2 D5 A5 C1 B4 A3 A2 D1 E3

E5 C3 B3 A3 A3 E2 D1 C4 A5 B3 C4 D2 D1 B2

B4 E2 C4 C3 A5 D5 B3 A2 C4 C3 B3 C4 A2 D1 E3

A5 B3 C4 D2 B2 D1 B1 B4 C4 A2 D1 E3

D3 B4 A3 A3 E5 E3 B2 A5 A3 A2 D5 B4 A5”

(A1 A5 E2 A5 E5 B4 E5 2: ___ - ___).

Now write it out and say it three times. Say it aloud morning, noon, and night.

EXAMINING THE EVIDENCE

"Look, Max! Look at Sam over there by the pit," laughed Molly.

"What is he doing?" replied a puzzled Max.

"It looks like he's onto a clue," whispered Molly. "Maybe we need to go check it out."

"Shhhh, Molly," whispered Max. "I'll try and sneak up on him so we can see what he's discovered. Stay here and be ready in case he decides to make a run for it."

"Aha! Gotcha, boy!" Max laughed. "What is in your mouth? What have you dug up this time, you wild pup?"

Molly and Uncle Jake ran toward Max and Sam to see Sam's latest find.

"Well, I'll be," Uncle Jake said as he pushed back his hat and squatted down to see Sam's find. "Sam has caught a gecko. I have never seen a dog that could catch lizards, but nothing you do should ever surprise me. Come on, boy. Let that gecko go and let's go get a doggie treat. Then we need to get started examining the evidence that we uncovered by digging up our key words. We need to ask some questions."

Archaeologists ask lots and lots of questions to help them understand what happened in the past. Let's practice this skill today by asking the 5 W's and an H questions. What are the 5 W's and an H? They are the WHO, WHAT, WHERE, WHEN, WHY, and HOW questions.

1. Asking WHO helps you find out:
   WHO wrote this?
   WHOM was it written to?
   WHOM are we reading about?
   WHO said this or did
   that?

2. WHAT helps you understand:
   WHAT is the author talking about?
   WHAT are the main things that happen?

3. WHERE helps you learn:
   WHERE did something happen?
   WHERE did they go?
   WHERE was this said?

   When we discover a "where" we double-underline the "where" in green.

4. WHEN tells us about time. We mark it with a green clock like this:
   WHEN tells us:
   WHEN did this event happen? Or WHEN will it happen?
   WHEN did the main characters do something? It helps us to follow the order of events, which is so important to an archaeologist.

5. WHY asks questions like:
   WHY did he say that?
   WHY did this happen?
   WHY did they go there?

6. HOW lets you figure out things like:
   HOW is something to be done?
   HOW did people know something had happened?

So let's get started asking questions by looking at the site. Turn to your Observation Worksheets on Genesis 2:15–3:24. Read Genesis 2:15-25 and answer the questions below.

Genesis 2:16-17 WHAT did God tell man about eating from the trees in the Garden of Eden?

you may eat from any tree except for the tree of knowledge, which you will surly die

Genesis 2:17 WHAT would happen to man if he broke God's commandment and ate from the tree of the knowledge of good and evil?

He would die

Up to this time, has anyone or anything died since God created the world? ___ Yes _✓_ No

No, we see that God created a perfect world and all that was in it was very good. At the close of Genesis 2 the world is still a perfect place. Let's read Genesis 3 and see what happens next.

Genesis 3:1 WHO approaches Eve in the garden?

The serpent

Genesis 3:1 WHAT was the serpent's question to Eve?

Has God asked you not to eat from any tree of the garden.

Genesis 3:2-3 Does Eve answer the serpent?
✓ Yes ___ No

Genesis 3:4-5 WHAT is the serpent's statement to Eve?
"You surely will not die!"

Did God say that they would die in Genesis 2:17?
✓ Yes ___ No

So, does the serpent contradict what God has said? (*Contradict* means to deny or to say the opposite of what is said.) ✓ Yes ___ No

Genesis 3:6 WHAT did the woman do?

She took fruit & ate it, then gave to her husband

WHOM did the woman believe: God or the serpent?

The serpent

Did Adam and Eve honor and obey God's commandment in Genesis 2:16-17? ✓ Yes ✓ No
then

If your answer is no, then WHAT did Adam and Eve do? Unscramble the answer in the parentheses and fill in the blanks. They d i s o b e y e d God. (bieodsyde)

HOW about you? Do you honor and obey what God says you should do in His Word? ✓ (try) Yes ___ No

HOW about obeying your parents? Do you do the things they tell you to do? ✓ Yes ___ No

Are you obedient or disobedient? I hope obedient

WHAT do you call disobedience—do you know? As we continue to dig deeper this week, we will uncover the evidence that shows us just what disobedience is and how it affects us.

Have you practiced saying your memory verse? Good work. Then let's climb out of the pit and go grab something good to eat at the mess tent. Digging makes us hungry. How about you?

Good morning, junior archaeologists! Are you ready to climb back down into the pit and scrape away the dirt so we can uncover more clues in Genesis 3? We need to be sure we uncover the evidence that shows us WHO the serpent is.

To take a closer look at the serpent and uncover his identity, we need to read Genesis 3. Let's make a list of what we see about the serpent.

The Serpent:

Genesis 3:1 The serpent was ______________________________
Genesis 3:13 "The serpent d _ _ _ _ _ _ _ me."
Genesis 3:14 The serpent is c _ _ _ _ _.
Genesis 3:15 _ _ _ _ _ _ between serpent and woman,
between her __________ and your __________.

Now let's do some cross-referencing. WHAT is cross-referencing? Cross-referencing is where we compare Scripture with Scripture by going to other passages in the Bible. This is a very important Bible study tool that we can use as we search out the meaning of Scripture because we know that Scripture never contradicts Scripture.

So let's read Revelation 12:9, which is printed out below:

> *And the great dragon was thrown down, the serpent of old who is called the devil and Satan, who deceives the whole world; he was thrown down to the earth, and his angels were thrown down with him.*

Now WHO is the great dragon? Write out the three names that tell us WHO the great dragon is.

a. ______________________________

b. ______________________________

c. ______________________________

Go back to the passage above on Revelation 12:9, and mark each reference to the great dragon and any pronouns and synonyms that go with it with a red pitchfork like this:

So WHO is the serpent? ______________________

Revelation 12:9 WHAT does the serpent do to the whole world? he decieves the whole world

WHAT does the word *deceive* mean? Look it up in a dictionary and write out what it means. trick

Look up and read 2 Corinthians 11:14. HOW does Satan disguise himself? (*Disguise* means to change your appearance so that you won't be recognized. It is to conceal or hide who you are.)

an angel of light

Now look up and read John 8:44.

HOW is Satan described in verse 44? WHAT are his character traits?

He was a murderer from the beginning.

He does not abode in the truth.

There is no truth in him.

He is a liar and the father of it.

Let's review what happened with Eve. Do we see these character traits of Satan in his encounter with Eve?

HOW does Satan approach Eve? Does he come right out and say, "Eve, don't listen to God; He's lying to you?" Or is he tricky, starting up a friendly conversation and slyly asking a question?

He is decieving

Genesis 3:1 WHAT is the question Satan asks Eve?

Has God forbbiden you from any tree

Is Satan a liar? Look at what Satan tells Eve in Genesis 3:4 and see if what Satan says contradicts (denies) what God says in Genesis 2:17.

Genesis 3:4 WHAT does Satan say?

"You surely will not die"

Genesis 2:17 WHAT did God say?

"If you eat from it you will surely die

Do Satan's words agree with God's words?
___ Yes ✓ No

Is Satan a liar? ✓ Yes ___ No

Look at Genesis 3:5 WHAT good thing does Satan make Eve think she is missing?

That you will know good & evil

Is Satan a deceiver? ✓ Yes ___ No

Now that we have uncovered the evidence on WHO Satan is and how he operates, we need to be careful that we aren't deceived by him.

Have you ever doubted something that God says in His Word is true? ___ Yes ✓ No

Are there times when you think that God is keeping something good from you? ___ Yes ✓ No

Have you ever been tricked into believing that something was good and then found out it wasn't?
___ Yes ✓ No

If you answered yes to any of these questions, then you have fallen into Satan's lies and have allowed him to deceive you. To keep from falling into Satan's trap, we need to remember three things:

1. WHO God is. We need to know His character and His goodness.

2. WHAT God's Word says. That's what you're doing right now by doing these Bible studies and learning God's Word. Knowing God's Word will keep you from being deceived by Satan and by the things the world tells us are okay but don't line up with what God's Word says.

3. Don't DOUBT God's judgment. We are to trust that God knows what is best for us at all times, even when it doesn't look like it to us. We are to trust Him. We walk by our faith in God—in who He is and not by the way things look.

Way to go! Let's climb out of the pit. Tomorrow we will find out more about Adam and Eve's disobedience.

SEARCHING FOR CLUES

"Hey, Max," Molly called out, "are you ready to go back down to the pit?"

"I sure am. Uncle Jake thinks we might be very close to a find. We scraped off a lot of dirt yesterday, and he's sure we'll discover something soon."

So, junior archaeologists, grab that *patish* and trowel and make your way back down into the pit. Let's continue to uncover the truth of what happened in the Garden of Eden.

We have discovered from marking key words and asking the 5 W's and an H that Adam and Eve disobeyed God. Do you know WHAT disobedience is? WHAT would you call it? Unscramble the word in the parentheses and place it in the blanks. S I N (nis)

WHAT is sin? HOW can we find out? To get started, we can do a word study on the word *sin*. A word study is where you look at the word you are studying in the original language it was written in. Did you know that the Old Testament (where Genesis is found) was written primarily in Hebrew with some Aramaic? And the New Testament was written in Koine Greek. So by looking at both the Hebrew (Old Testament) and Greek (New Testament) words for *sin,* we will understand more about what the word *sin* means. Check out Max and Molly's field notebook below to discover the Hebrew and Greek words for *sin* and what they mean.

> The Hebrew word for *sin* is *chata*, which is pronounced khaw-taw' and means "to miss the mark, the way," or "to fail, to go wrong."
>
> The Greek word for *sin* is *hamartia* pronounced ham-ar-tee'-ah, which means "a missing of the mark, error."

From what we have studied in Genesis 1–3, did God give Adam and Eve a command? Did He set a standard for them? ✓ Yes ___ No

WHAT was that command? Write it out below.

Not to eat or touch the tree of

Knowledge

Did Adam and Eve fail, miss the mark, or go wrong? ✓ Yes ___ No

So according to the Hebrew and Greek definitions, would you say that Adam and Eve sinned when they disobeyed God? ✓ Yes ___ No

Now let's dig a little deeper and see what else we can learn about sin. Let's do some cross-referencing and see what the Bible says sin is.

Look up and read 1 John 3:4. According to 1 John 3:4, WHAT is sin?

sin is the transgression of the law

Look up and read 1 John 5:17. WHAT does this verse say sin is?

all unrighteousness is sin, there is a sin not unto death

Read James 4:17. WHAT is sin?

knoweth no good & doeth not, to him it is sin

Read Romans 14:23. WHAT is sin?

for whatever is not of faith, is sin

Now let's take it verse by verse. We see from Scripture that: Sin is lawlessness.

Did Adam and Eve break God's law? _✓_ Yes ___ No

Sin is unrighteousness. Unrighteousness is *not* doing what God says is right. It is doing what God says is wrong.

Did Adam and Eve do something God said was wrong? _✓_ Yes ___ No

Sin is also knowing the right thing to do and not doing it.

Did Adam and Eve know the right thing to do? _✓_ Yes ___ No

Did they do the right thing? ___ Yes _✓_ No

Sin is whatever is not from faith. Faith is believing God and taking Him at His Word.

Did Adam and Eve believe what God told them, or did they believe someone else? Did they take God at His Word?

They believed the serpent. No.

So WHAT causes us to sin? WHERE does sin come from? Let's look at the root of sin. Look up and read Isaiah 53:6.

HOW are we like sheep?

We have gone astray.

Each of us has one to his own way.

This verse shows us that the root of all sin begins with us. It's when we do what we want to do instead of what God wants us to do. Just like the sheep, we each turn to our own way. Adam and Eve chose to do what they wanted, what they thought was right, instead of what God told them was right.

WHAT made them do that? We'll find out more tomorrow as we continue to look at the clues we have uncovered in Genesis 3. You are doing a great job at uncovering the layers one at a time. Keep up the good work!

READING THE MAP

"Mmmm, that sure was good, wasn't it, Sam?" Max asked, patting Sam on the head. Uncle Jake walked up and sat down next to Molly.

"I thought you guys might like a little break from the pit today. Why don't you pack a lunch and take Sam on a scouting expedition? You can explore some of the areas close by that you haven't seen yet. How does that sound?"

"Fantastic!" shouted Molly and Max at the same time.

"Good. Here's a map. I marked your boundaries here, in red. Don't go any farther than these boundaries. And one other thing," cautioned Uncle Jake, "stay out of any caves! Caves can be very dangerous. Take your map and compass, stay together, and don't go where?"

"Into any caves," replied an impatient Max. "We got it, Uncle Jake. Let's go pack our lunch, Molly."

Sounds like fun, doesn't it? As we head off with Max and Molly, let's think about all we have discovered in the pit this week.

The clues we have uncovered have shown us who the serpent is, how he operates, and what sin is.

But WHAT led to Adam and Eve's sin? We know the root of sin is turning our own way. But Adam and Eve lived in a perfect world and had a wonderful relationship with God. WHY would they choose their way over God's? WHAT happened?

Let's find out. Let's spend some time with our "site boss" and then head back to Genesis 3 on page 192 to Eve and the serpent. Read Genesis 3:1-5 to put yourself in context. Now read verse 6 and look at Eve's actions. WHAT does she do? Circle the action verbs that show what Eve does in verse 6.

Just to make sure you know what an action verb is, check out Max and Molly's verb map below.

VERB MAP

Did you know that every sentence has a verb? A verb is a word that usually shows action. But a verb can also show state of being, it can help another verb, and sometimes a verb will link a word in the predicate to the subject in a sentence.

Let's look at an action verb. An action verb tells what the person or thing in the sentence is doing, such as "Sam digs lots of holes."

Digs is the action verb in the sentence because it shows what Sam does.

Now circle the action verbs in Genesis 3:6 on page 192.

WHAT three things led up to Eve eating the fruit?

a. Eve s a w.

b. She t o o k.

c. She a t e.

After Eve ate the fruit, she did another action. WHAT was it?

She g a v e also to her husband.

And WHAT did her husband do? He a t e.

Genesis 3:7 And WHAT happened after they ate of the fruit?

Their eyes were opened

So WHY would Adam and Eve do what God said is wrong? WHAT did Satan do that led Eve to sin? We know he deceived Eve, but he did something else also. Satan tempted Eve to do what God had told her not to do.

WHAT is temptation? Let's find out. First let's check out Max and Molly's field notebook to find out what the Hebrew and Greek words are for *temptation.*

> The Hebrew word for *temptation* is *nasah,* and it is pronounced naw-saw', and it means "to test, try, prove."
> The Greek word *peirazo* is pronounced pi-rad'-zo, and it means "to entice, to lure, to entrap."

Now let's look at some cross-references that tell us more about temptation and being tempted.

Look up and read James 1:13-15.

James 1:13 Does God tempt anyone?

NO ?

James 1:14 HOW are you tempted?

drawn away from own lust, & enticed

James 1:15 WHAT does lust give birth to?

Sin

James 1:15 WHAT does sin bring forth?

death

Did God tempt Eve? ____ Yes ✓ No

James shows us very clearly that being tempted does not come from God. God does not tempt anyone. Temptation comes from being carried away and enticed by our own lust (our desires).

Let's compare WHAT happened to Eve to WHAT happens to a man named Achan in the Old Testament Book of Joshua. In Joshua 6 we see the fall of Jericho and God's instructions for taking the spoils of war. Look up and read Joshua 6:15-19.

Joshua 6:17 WHAT is God's command to the children of Israel about the city, Jericho, when they conquer it?

? accursed

Joshua 6:18 WHAT would happen if they took anything under the ban?

They would be accursed & the city cursed

Now read Joshua 7:1-26.

Joshua 7:1 WHAT did Achan do?

He took the acursed thing

HOW did God feel about this?

angry

Joshua 7:20-21 WHAT were the three actions that Achan said he did?

a. Achan saw a beautiful mantle, 200 shekels of silver, and a bar of gold 50 shekels in weight.

b. Achan coveted them.

c. Achan took them.

Joshua 7:20 WHAT does Achan say about his actions? "Truly, I have Sinned against God."

Does WHAT Achan did sound like what Eve did?

Similar

Did you notice how in both Achan's and Eve's situation that one action led to another?

First they were both tempted by what they s _a_ _w_.

It looked so good. Achan saw the beautiful mantle, and Eve saw that the fruit on the tree was a delight to the eyes. They were tempted, enticed, and lured by what they saw.

WHAT happened next? In Genesis 3:6 it says the woman s _a_ _w_ the tree was good for food, and that it was a delight for the eyes, and the tree was WHAT?
___desired___ to make one ___wise___

Look at Achan's second action in Joshua 7:21.

He c _o_ _v_ _e_ _t_ _e_ d. That means he desired it, it attracted him, and he wanted it very badly.

So we see that Achan and Eve didn't just look. They continued to look. They focused on what God had told them was forbidden.

So WHAT did continuing to look on what was forbidden lead to?

WHAT was both Eve's and Achan's next action? They t _o_ _o_ k.

So WHEN did Eve and Achan sin? Did it happen when they looked or when they took?

___Both, but mostly when they took___

WHY do you think that?

___Because coveting & taking are both___
___sins___

So is it a sin to be tempted? No way! Temptation is a lure, an enticement that comes from within. When a fisherman wants to catch a fish, does he cast an empty hook into the water? No, a fisherman thinks about what kind of fish he wants to catch, and then he puts a lure on his hook that will entice that fish. He chooses the bait that the fish will not be able to resist. He baits his hook and casts it in the water to entice the fish to swallow his hook. Once the fish gives in to temptation and goes for the bait, it is caught!

Satan does the same thing to us. He lures us with the things we think we have to have: movies we want to see and places we want to go. He entices us with our desires. Sin happens when we are carried away by our own lust (desires) and choose what we want over what God says is right. Sin happens when we act, when we do the wrong thing. Eve and Achan didn't sin by being tempted but by giving in to temptation and disobeying God.

We all will have temptations, but sin is a choice we make. One of the most important things that we need to remember is what we uncovered in James 1:13: God does not tempt anyone. God may allow you to be tempted, but He hates sin and never tempts anyone.

By the way, do you know how to handle temptations so that you don't sin? We'll uncover what God's Word tells us about how to deal with temptations next week.

Did you remember to say your memory verse to a friend or a grown-up? Why don't you do that right now? One of the best weapons we have to stand firm against temptations is to know God's Word.

3

GENESIS 3

Last week we began carefully digging up the evidence of what happened in the Garden of Eden to change it from the perfect place that God had created. As we continue to explore Genesis 3, we need to find out what happened next. WHAT did Adam and Eve do? WHAT were the consequences of sin?

But before we get started looking for new evidence, let's find out how we can handle temptations so that we don't sin.

A NEW DISCOVERY

"Hey, Max!" Molly shouted. "Look at that!"

"Wow!" Max stood looking amazed at the opening in the side of the mountain. "A real cave. I can't believe we actually found a real cave." Max walked up to the side of the mountain, ran his hand over the wall, and stuck his head in the opening, trying to see what was inside.

"No, Max!" Molly cried out. "Remember what Uncle Jake said: No caves."

"I know, Molly, I know. But what do you think is in there?" Max asked as he peeked around the opening. "There could be all kinds of cool stuff inside."

"Yeah, but Uncle Jake said it could be very dangerous," Molly reminded Max.

"Well, it doesn't look dangerous. See—it's just a big opening. We could go in just a little ways and take a quick look."

"I don't think we should, Max. Uncle Jake said, 'No caves.'"

"Okay, Molly. We won't go in since you're chicken!"

"No, I'm not, Max!" Molly was mad now. "I'll just take Sam and go look around the other side. We'll meet you back here in about five minutes."

"All right. See you and Sam in about five minutes."

As Molly and Sam headed around the corner, Max took another look at the cave. "What would it hurt if I just went in for a minute?"

Well, junior archaeologists, it looks like Max has run straight into a BIG temptation. HOW will he handle it? HOW should you handle temptations when they come your way? We need to find out. Let's use our map (the Bible) to find out how God tells us to handle temptations.

Look up the following Scriptures and answer the questions to solve the crossword puzzle on page 47.

Read Hebrews 4:14-16.

1. (Across) WHO was tempted in all things as we are, yet did not sin? Jesus

Isn't that amazing? Jesus was tempted just like we are, only He didn't sin. This should encourage us to know that we are not alone. Jesus knows just how we feel because He was tempted, too!

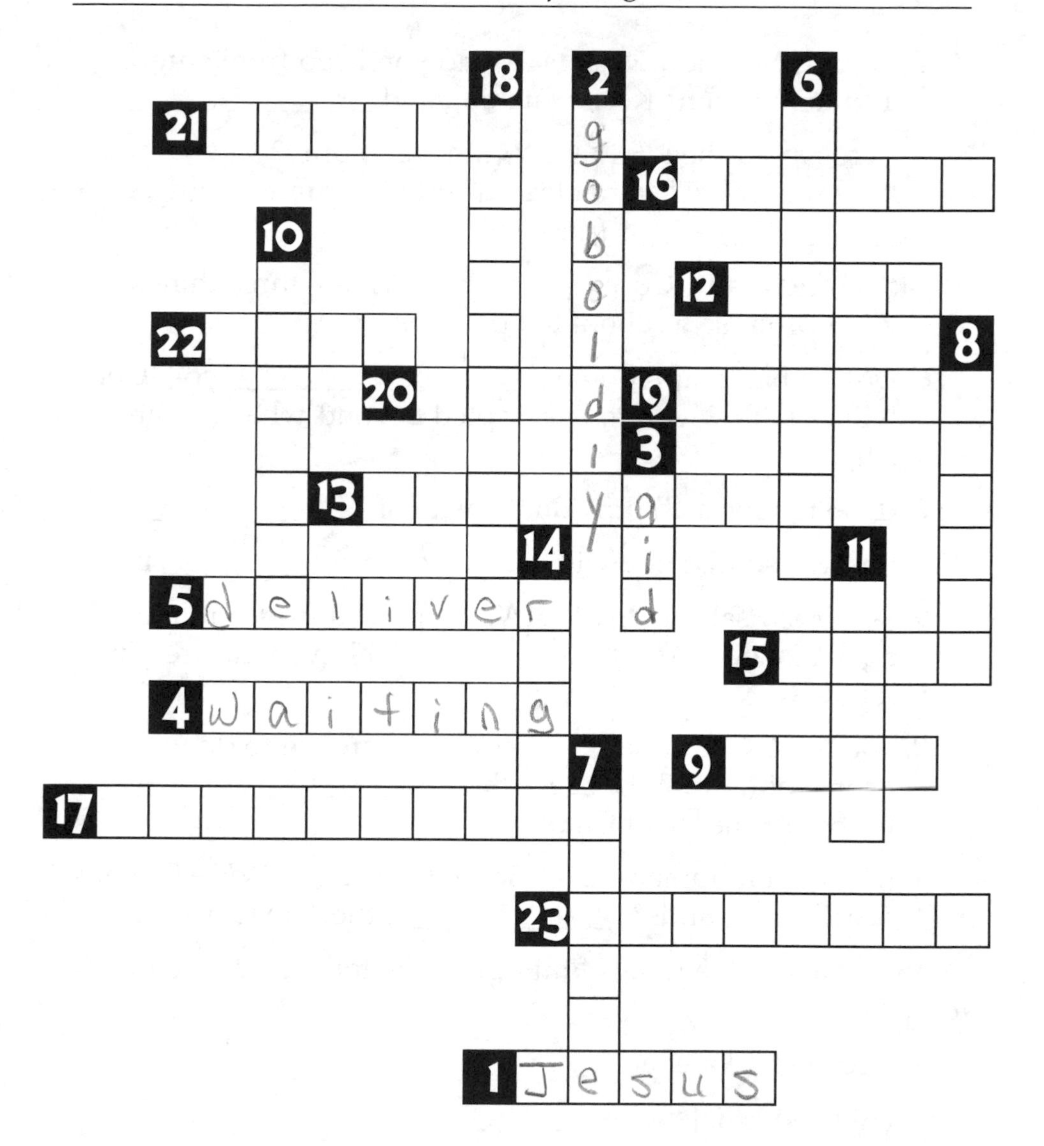

2. (Down) Hebrews 4:16 HOW do we find mercy and grace in our time of need?

   ___go___ ___bodly___ with confidence to the throne of grace to find help in time of need. (Put the answers from both blanks together on your crossword.)

3. (Down) Hebrews 2:17-18 Jesus is able to do WHAT? Come to the ___aid___ of those who are tempted.

4. Across) Matthew 26:41 HOW do you keep from entering into temptation? Keep watching and ________________.

5. Across) Matthew 6:13 HOW are we to pray?
Pray this way: "Do not lead us into temptation, but ______________ us from evil."

Look up and read 1 Corinthians 10:13. WHAT three things does God promise us about temptations?

6. Down) No temptation has ____taken____ you. God will not allow you to be tempted beyond what you are able.

7. (Down) God will provide the way of ______________

8. (Down) so that you will be able to ______________ it.

9. (Across) Psalm 119:11 WHAT keeps you from sinning against God? "Your ______________ I have treasured in my heart."

10. (Down) 2 Corinthians 10:3-5 WHAT are we to do with every thought? Take every thought ________________ to the obedience of Christ.

11. (Down) Philippians 4:7-8 God tells us to do WHAT to our hearts and minds? ______________ them in Christ Jesus.

Now write out the things Philippians 4:8 tells us we are to dwell on:

12. (Across) Whatever is ______________

13. (Across) Whatever is ______________

14. (Down) Whatever is ______________

15. (Across) Whatever is ______________

16. (Across) Whatever is ______________

17. (Across) Whatever is of __________ ______________, if there is any 18. (Down) __________________ and if anything is worthy of 19. (Across) ______________, dwell on these things.

2 Timothy 2:22 WHAT are we to do?

20. (Across) ______________ youthful lusts.
21. (Across) ______________ righteousness, faith, love, and peace.
22. (Across) Galatians 5:16 HOW do we keep from carrying out the desires of the flesh? ____________ by the Spirit.
23. (Across) Job 31:1 WHAT did Job do with his eyes? Made a _______________ with my eyes.

WHAT does that mean? That means Job made a treaty, a pact, a promise with his eyes. He was going to be careful about what he looked at.

Job recognized the danger in looking: The looking could lead to acting. He chose to be careful about what he looked at.

HOW about you?

WHAT books and magazines do you read? WHAT movies do you watch? And WHAT video games do you play?

Are you careful about what you look at?
_√_ Yes ___ No

Are you careful with the friends that you choose to hang out with and the places that you go?
_√_ Yes ___ No

HOW do you know if a movie, a book, or a place is okay? Take it and measure it up to God's standard. Philippians 4:8 it. Ask yourself: Is this movie, picture, or video true, honorable, right, pure, lovely, of good repute, is there any excellence in it, anything worthy of praise?

If it fails God's test, then maybe you need to make a covenant with your eyes and not look at it. Remember, continuing to dwell on (to look at) what God had said was forbidden is the action that led to Achan's and Eve's sin, and their death.

Now examine yourself. Write out a way that you have been tempted.

____

____

Did you handle this temptation God's way, or did you sin?

____

HOW should you handle temptation the next time it happens?

____

____

Write out a prayer to God, asking Him to keep you from temptations, to come to your aid, and to help you make a covenant with your eyes.

____

____

____

____

Remember, we are not alone. We do not have to handle temptations by ourselves. We have God's Word. That's what Jesus used when Satan tempted Him (Matthew 4:1-11). God has given us His promise that He will provide a way of escape and will help us endure the temptation. We need to remember to run to Him and ask Him for His help.

> WHAT are you to do with youthful lusts (2 Timothy 2:22)? _______________ them.

Don't forget that when you find yourself with friends who are doing the wrong thing or in a place you shouldn't be. Remember this verse and flee!

That was some great exploring of your heart! Now let's take a look at Molly and Max's map to discover your memory verse for the week.

Each word on Max and Molly's map is spelled with a different font. A font is a type of print. Some of the letters in the words on the map are underlined. To discover your memory verse, you need to look at the font of the letters that go with the blanks under the map. Then go to the map and find the font in the words on the map that match it. Place the underlined letters of the font that matches in the empty blanks to form a new word.

Once you have matched all the fonts, you will have revealed this week's verse. Write it out on an index card, and then say it out loud three times each day.

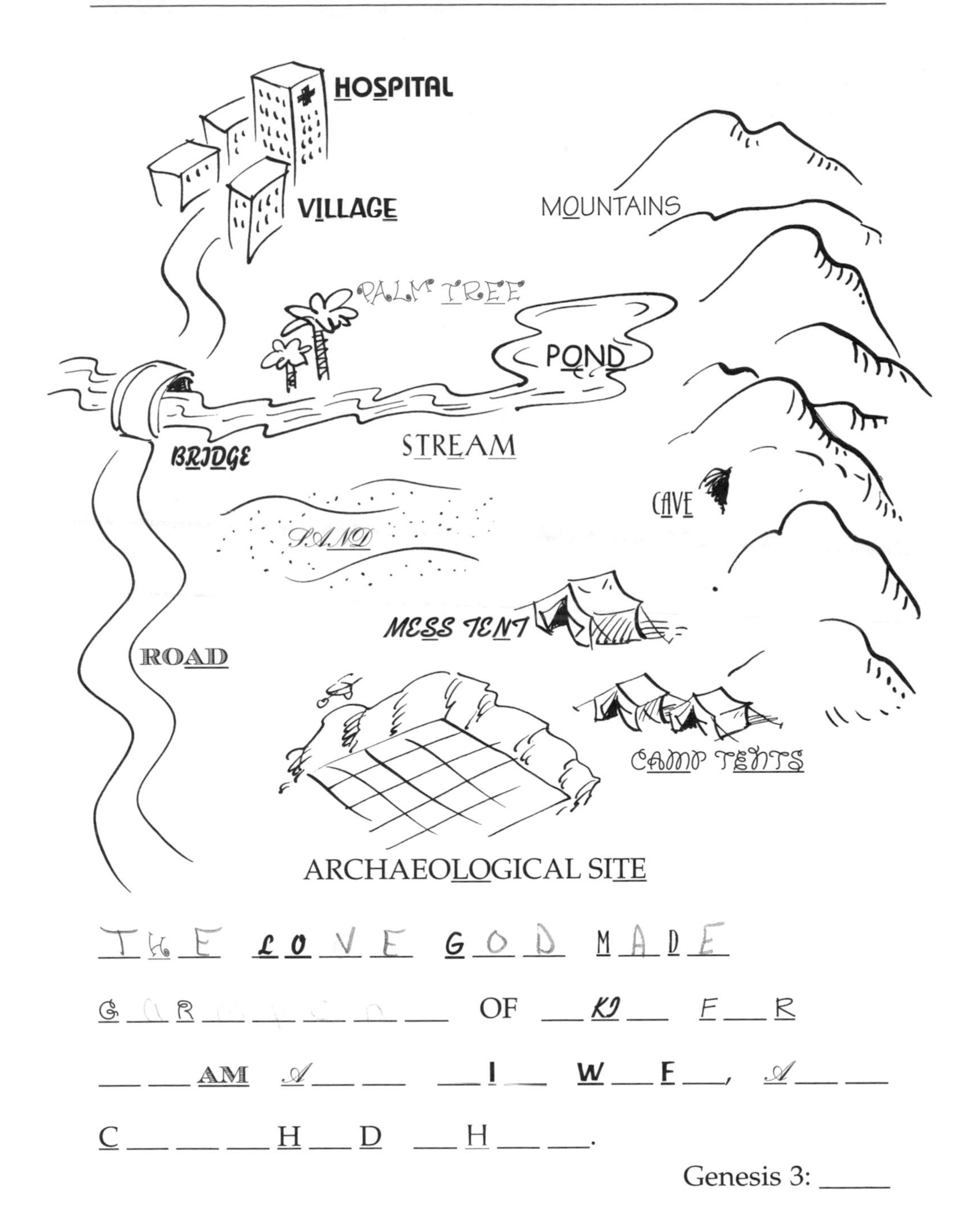
HOSPITAL
VILLAGE
MOUNTAINS
PALM TREE
POND
BRIDGE
STREAM
CAVE
SAND
MESS TENT
ROAD
CAMP TENTS
ARCHAEOLOGICAL SITE
T H E L O V E G O D M A D E
G _ R _ _ _ _ _ _ OF _ KI _ F _ R
_ _ AM A _ _ _ I _ W _ F _, A _ _
C _ _ _ H _ D _ H _ _.
Genesis 3: _____

THE SEARCH IS ON

"Uncle Jake, Uncle Jake!" Molly ran toward camp with tears streaming down her face and Sam barking at her heels.

Uncle Jake rushed toward Molly. "Molly, what's wrong? Why are you crying? Sam, stop that! Quit barking! Settle down, boy. Okay, Molly, take a breath and tell me what's wrong."

"Oh, Uncle Jake, Max and I found a cave, right about here," Molly said as she showed him the map. "Max wanted to go in, but I reminded him that you said no, and he called me a chicken. Can you believe it? I am not chicken!"

"Hmmmm, I think I get the picture."

"No, you don't, Uncle Jake. I was mad so I told Max that I would take Sam and look around the other side of the cave. We planned to meet back at the cave in five minutes, but he wasn't there!"

"Maybe he just wandered off. How long has he been gone?"

"About 30 minutes. I looked all around for him. Uncle Jake, do you think he went into the cave by himself?"

"I don't know, Molly. Max usually obeys. But then again, exploring a cave can be very tempting. I better get a search crew together. Why don't you go get the first aid kit, flashlights, ropes, and water while I go talk to the team?"

Well, junior archaeologists, it looks like Max is missing. Let's join the dig team as they pray for Max and his safety, and then we'll be ready to head out with the search crew.

We need to go to Genesis 3 on page 192. Now that we know Adam and Eve were tempted and disobeyed God, let's see WHAT happened next.

Read Genesis 3 and answer the 5 W's and an H.

Genesis 3:7 WHAT happened after they ate the fruit?

____

Looking back at Genesis 2:25, were the man and woman ashamed at being naked? ___ Yes ___ No

WHAT do you think happened to make them feel different about being naked?

____

____

Genesis 3:8 WHAT did the man and woman do when they heard the sound of God walking in the garden?

____

WHY do you think they hid?

____

____

Genesis 3:9 WHAT did God say?

____

Since the Bible tells us that God knows everything, do you think He didn't know where Adam and Eve were? ___ Yes ___ No

WHY do you think God asked Adam where he was?

____

____

Genesis 3:10 WHY did the man hide?

____

Have you ever hidden something you have done from your parents? ___ Yes ___ No

Genesis 3:11 WHAT two questions did God ask?

a. ______________________________

b. ______________________________

Since God knows what Adam and Eve have done, WHY does He ask Adam these questions?

____

____

Genesis 3:12 WHAT was the man's response to God?

____

Genesis 3:12 When Adam is questioned, WHAT does he do first: admit (confess) what he did or blame someone else?

____

Genesis 3:13 WHAT was the woman's response to God?

____

How about you? When you do something wrong, do you confess that you are guilty, or do you look for someone to blame, like a brother or a sister?

____

Look up and read 1 John 1:9. WHAT does God tell us we are to do when we sin?

____

WHAT happens when we confess our sins?

____

____

To confess our sins is to agree with God that what we did was wrong. We do not try to hide what we did. Do you see why God asked Adam and Eve what they did? God is a God of mercy and forgiveness. He was giving Adam and Eve a chance to tell Him they had done something wrong.

Genesis 3:14 WHAT did God do to the serpent?

a. c __ __ __ __ __ the serpent

b. Told the serpent, "On your ___________ you will go."

c. God told the serpent He would "put______________ between you and the _____________, and between your ________ and her __________; He shall ___________ you on the ____________, and you shall ____________ him on the ____________."

Genesis 3:16 WHAT did God say to the woman?

"I will ______________ ____________________ your __________ in ____________________."

"Your husband...will ___________ over ___________."

Genesis 3:17-19 WHAT did God say to the man?

____

So were there consequences from disobeying God?
___ Yes ___ No

Absolutely! Tomorrow we will continue to look at the awful consequences of sin, and not only what it cost Adam and Eve, but also what it cost the whole world.

As you practice saying your memory verse, think about why God made these garments of skin. We'll find out as we continue to dig up truth in God's Word.

A RESCUE MISSION

"Right over here," directed Molly as the search crew and Uncle Jake approached the cave.

"Molly, I want you to wait out here with Ben and Sam. William, Mary Frances, and I will go into the cave to see if we can find Max. If we aren't back in 30 minutes, Ben, I want you to radio the rescue squad."

As Uncle Jake, Mary Frances, and William turned on their flashlights, they cautiously entered the dark cave, calling Max's name.

"Look at all these passageways," said Mary Frances. "Which way do you think he went?"

"I think I see a few footprints over here," answered Uncle Jake. "Let's try following this passageway."

"Max," called Uncle Jake as he continued into the cave. "Max, can you hear me?"

"Over here, I'm over here," Max tried to yell, but his throat was so dry he could barely get the words out. "Down here," he tried one more time.

"Wait a minute, I think I heard something." Mary Frances grabbed Uncle Jake by the arm. "Listen."

Uncle Jake, Mary Frances, and William stood quietly and listened. They could barely hear Max's faint voice.

"Where do you think it's coming from?" asked William.

"I'm not sure," replied Uncle Jake.

As they continued to search, Mary Frances turned a corner and shone her flashlight along the side of the cave as she called for Max. Startled by a faint sound, Mary Frances jumped and started moving toward the sound. As she took the next step, her foot met nothing but air. "Oh, no!" Mary Frances cried out as she lost her balance. She reached out to stop herself from falling and grabbed onto a big rock, knocking dirt and pebbles over the edge of a steep drop-off. While Mary Frances was pulling herself up and catching her breath, she saw Uncle Jake and William rushing her way. "Wait, guys!" she called out. "Slow down. There's a drop-off right in front of my feet. I thought I heard Max calling and almost stepped right over the edge." Mary Frances was shaking.

"Do you think Max could have fallen off the edge?" asked a concerned Uncle Jake.

"I don't know. Why don't we lie on our stomachs and slide up to the edge of the drop-off and shine our flashlights over the side?"

As the search for Max continues, we can see that his disobedience has put his life and the search crew's lives in danger. Let's go back to Genesis and continue looking at what sin cost Adam and Eve.

Read Genesis 2:17.

WHAT did God say would happen if they ate from the tree?

____

Did they die? ___________

That's a hard question, isn't it? Because no, their bodies didn't die physically the moment they ate the fruit. But there was an immediate spiritual death for Adam and Eve. They were no longer pure and sinless. In Genesis 2 they were not ashamed of their nakedness, but after they sinned they sewed fig leaves together, made loin coverings, and hid from God. We see that their relationship with God was immediately changed.

Let's look up and read Romans 5:12.

HOW did sin enter the world?

____

From what we have learned in Genesis 3, WHO is the one man?

____

WHAT came through sin?

____

WHERE did death spread?

____

WHY does death spread to all men?

____

Romans shows us that once sin enters the world through Adam, then every human being born after that time is born a sinner. Look up and read Romans 3:23. WHO has sinned? ____

That word *all* means everyone. So were you born a sinner? ___ Yes ___ No

Even if you try to be good and do good things, are you still a sinner? ___ Yes ___ No

HOW do you know?

____

____

We see once again that the consequence of sin is death. Go to Genesis 3 on page 193 and read Genesis 3:14-24.

Genesis 3:21 WHAT did God make to clothe Adam and Eve?

____

HOW did God get the skins for the garments?

____

Did something die in order to cover Adam and Eve after they sinned? ___ Yes ___ No

From the beginning of Creation up until now, has any living creature ever died? ___ Yes ___ No

Until man sinned there was no shedding of blood, no death. Adam and Eve lived in a perfect world. But once they sinned, death entered the world and something had to die to cover their sins. Let's compare Scripture with Scripture. Look up and read Hebrews 9:22.

WHAT has to be done in order for there to be forgiveness?

____

In Genesis 3, God kills an animal to cover Adam and Eve, but an animal can never take away our sins completely. Look up and read Hebrews 9:11-12. HOW are our sins forgiven?

____

So when God killed an animal by shedding its blood and covering Adam and Eve with its skins, He was covering their sins until the perfect sacrifice would be made. The perfect, unblemished Lamb of God, Jesus Christ, would come to earth as a baby, grow up, live a sinless life, and die on a cross to take away the sins of the whole world forever.

That's why we do not have to sacrifice animals for sin anymore. The animal sacrifices were a picture of what Jesus would do for us when He died on the cross. What God did for Adam and Eve was a temporary solution to cover sin until, in God's perfect timing, He would send a Savior, the Lord Jesus Christ, whose blood would take away our sins forever. Isn't that awesome? God loves us so much that even though we are sinners, He provides a way so that we can live with Him forever.

Now let's head back to the cave to help the search crew look for Max. Tomorrow we will look at a very special passage in Genesis that shows us God's first promise of our salvation.

RESCUED AT LAST

Uncle Jake, Mary Frances, and William started crawling very slowly toward the edge of the drop-off.

Uncle Jake reached the edge first and shone his flashlight over the side. "Max, Max, are you down there?" Uncle Jake felt a moment of panic as his flashlight shone on Max sitting on a small ledge about five feet below the drop-off.

"Yuck!" Max spit dirt out of his mouth to answer his uncle. "I just got a bunch of dirt in my mouth and face, but I think I'm okay."

"Just stay still. I'm going to send a rope down. Slide it over your head and tighten it around your waist, and then we'll pull you up."

Uncle Jake handed Mary Frances and William one end of the rope, and they backed themselves up until they were at the far wall of the cave where they could safely stand up. In the meantime, Uncle Jake looped the other end of the rope for Max to slide over his head.

"Yeowwww!" screamed Max.

Mary Frances jumped, and Uncle Jake quickly looked over the side. "What happened, Max?"

"I think something bit me," cried Max as a stinging pain shot through his leg. "I can't really see without the flashlight. Oh man, it hurts! Uncle Jake, please hurry and get me out of here!"

"Here comes the rope, Max. Put it around you. Good. Now tighten it and hang on." Uncle Jake yelled at William and Mary Frances, "Start pulling. Let's get him off that ledge."

As William and Mary Frances started pulling the rope to lift Max off the ledge, Uncle Jake spied a fat-tailed scorpion scampering away. Uncle Jake reached out and pulled Max to safety. "Max, show me where it hurts."

"Oh, Uncle Jake," whispered Mary Frances as she saw Max's leg. "What do you think stung him? His leg is beginning to swell."

Uncle Jake looked at Max. "Max, I saw a scorpion on the ledge, and your leg looks like you've been stung. I am going to carry you back to the Jeep. We need to get you to the hospital."

"I'm sorry, Uncle Jake," Max cried. "I really messed up this time."

"It's all right, Max. We'll talk about it later, okay? William, why don't you lead the way with your flashlight so I can carry Max."

Molly looked up to see William, Mary Frances, and Uncle Jake carrying Max as they came out of the cave. "Look, Ben, they just came out. Oh, no. Uncle Jake is carrying Max."

"I'm sure he's okay, Molly. Just don't let Sam loose."

"Ben," Uncle Jake called out, "radio the hospital. Tell them that a fat-tailed scorpion has stung Max and we are on our way. Molly, climb into the Jeep and hold onto Sam. We need to hurry. This is serious. Time is critical with this kind of bite. Let's go!"

As our search crew is racing to the hospital to save Max's life, let's take a look at a very special passage in Genesis 3:15. Turn to page 193 and read Genesis 3:15.

WHO is there enmity (that means hatred) between?

____

____

Seed means "child" or "offspring."

WHO is going to be bruised on the head?

____

WHO will be bruised on the heel?

____

WHO is the woman's seed? Do you know? We can trace Adam's generations all the way to Abraham by reading Luke 3:34-38.

Now look up and read Galatians 3:16. WHO is Abraham's seed?

____

Did you know there is only one way to die that bruises a person's heel? The only death that causes the heel to be bruised is crucifixion. WHOM does Satan hate? WHO was crucified (bruised on the heel) for our sins?

____

Satan bruised Jesus on the heel (the crucifixion), but Jesus will bruise Satan on the head. Did you know that being bruised on the head is a fatal blow? It shows a total defeat.

> Look up and read Revelation 20:10. WHAT happens to Satan?
>
> ____
>
> For HOW long? ________________________________

So do you know why Genesis 3:15 is such a special passage? This passage is called the *protevangelium.* Have you ever heard that word before? *Prot* means "the first." Now can you think of a word that *evangelium* looks like? How about *evangelism?* Evangelism is teaching the gospel.

Genesis 3:15 is called the *protevangelium* because it is the first promise in the Bible of man's salvation through Jesus Christ. It is a passage of hope. In Genesis, after man falls, we see God promising a redeemer who will save us from sin and death. Jesus is that redeemer. That means He will pay the price for our sins.

> Have you put your trust in Jesus to save you from your sins? ___ Yes ___ No
>
> Or are you trusting in how good you are?
> ___ Yes ___ No

Remember, we can never be good enough. We are *all* sinners. And there is only one way to be cleansed from sin, and that is through the shedding of Jesus' blood.

But that's not all. God also promises that Jesus will bruise the serpent's head. One day soon Satan will be totally defeated and thrown into the lake of fire forever and ever! And those who have trusted Jesus as their Savior will reign with Him in a new heaven and earth where sin and death have been abolished. Isn't that exciting? Do you ever think about what the new heaven and earth will be like? God tells us right in His Word. (If you want to take a sneak peek to see the new heaven and earth, you can find it described in Revelation 21:1–22:5.)

Let's finish up Genesis 3. Turn to page 194 and read Genesis 3:20-24.

Genesis 3:22-24 WHAT happened to Adam and Eve?

____

Genesis 3:22 WHY?

____

____

Genesis 3:24 WHO guarded the way to the tree of life?

____

WHY do you think God doesn't want Adam and Eve to eat from the tree of life? ___________________________

Do you think God was punishing them or protecting them? ____________________________________

Is God loving or mean? ___________________________

We have already seen how loving and merciful God is. God has promised Adam and Eve a Savior and sacrificed an animal to cover them. Why would He send them out of the garden? To protect them. If they ate from the tree of life, they would live in a sinful condition and be separated from God forever.

Now think about your relationship with your parents. Have your parents ever kept you from going somewhere or doing something that you really wanted to do? ___ Yes ___ No

Did you think that your mom and dad were being mean and unreasonable when they said no? ___ Yes ___ No

From looking at God's love and protection of Adam and Eve, do you see how much your mom and dad really love you and only want what is best for you?

God has sent Adam and Eve out of the garden so they cannot eat of the tree of life and live forever. Let's take a look at Genesis 5:5 on page 199 to see WHEN Adam died.

HOW old was Adam when he died? ____________ years

Let's make a list to contrast what creation was like *before* the fall of man to what creation was like *after* the fall of man.

A contrast shows us how things are different or opposite. Good and bad, black and white, and night and day are all contrasts. Fill in the blanks in the lists below to show the difference in the world *before* the fall and *after* the fall.

Before the Fall	**After the Fall**
1. Genesis 1:31 God saw all of creation and it was very ________. No s __ __.	1. S __ __ entered the world.
2. _______ and _______ were with God in the garden.	2. Adam and Eve h __ __ from God.
3. Genesis 2:25 N __ __ __ d, not ashamed	3. Genesis 3:7-8 Knew they were n __ __ __ d, ________ themselves
4. Tree of life, no d __ __ __ h	4. Animals and man __________.
5. Genesis 2:15 Keep the g __ __ __ __ __	5. Genesis 3:23 s __ __ __ from the garden
6. No curse, it was very ________ Genesis 2:16 From any	6. Gen. 3:17-18 C __ __ __ __ d is the g __ __ __ __ d. Both t __ __ __ __ __ and

Before the Fall

t___ ___ ___ of
the garden they may
__ __ __ freely, except
from the tree of the
knowledge of ________
and ________.

After the Fall

t __ __ __ __ __ __ __ it
would grow for them. In
t __ __ l and s __ __ __ t
they will eat.

Now draw a picture in the divided box below. On the left side, show how creation looked before the fall, and on the right side, show how it looked after the fall.

Before the Fall **After the Fall**

Great work!

A SPECIAL ASSIGNMENT

"Uncle Jake," exclaimed Molly, "what's wrong? What's happening to Max?"

"It's okay, Molly." Mary Frances reached over and took Molly by the hand. "Max is having a convulsion. Sometimes a scorpion sting can cause convulsions and frothing at the mouth. Why don't we pray together? The hospital isn't far now."

As the Jeep pulled up to the emergency room door, Uncle Jake hopped out and rushed inside, carrying a very sick Max. "I have an 11-year-old boy with a fat-tailed scorpion sting, and he's having convulsions."

"Let me get a nurse, then I'll page Dr. Vick," replied the lady at the front desk. Nurse Hobbs quickly arrived with a gurney and wheeled Max into Room 3 as they paged Dr. Vick.

Twenty minutes later Dr. Vick came out and said to Uncle Jake and the others, "We had to give Max a shot of antivenin, but he's going to be just fine. It's a blessing that you saw the scorpion. Knowing what stung him allowed us to treat him quickly and probably saved his life. You can go see him once we get him settled in. We need to keep him overnight for observation. Then if he continues to do well, you can take him back to the campsite tomorrow."

Whew! Are you relieved? Max is going to be okay. However, while he's resting in the hospital, Uncle Jake has a special assignment for you. Let's take a closer look at Adam and Eve's relationship.

Turn to page 190 and read Genesis 2:18-25.

Genesis 2:18 WHAT did God make for man?

____

Genesis 2:18 WHY did God say man needed a helper?

____

Genesis 2:21-22 HOW did God create woman?

____

Genesis 2:22 WHAT did God do as soon as He finished creating woman?

____

Genesis 2:23 WHY did Adam call her "woman"?

____

Isn't that awesome how God knows exactly what we need? God knew that man needed a helper, someone suitable just for him. So He created woman and brought her to the man. WHAT happens next? God has a very special relationship planned for them. Let's take a look as God creates the very first marriage.

Genesis 2:24 WHAT three things was the man to do when he married?

____

____

____

God told the man to leave his mother and father and to cleave to his wife. WHAT does *cleave* mean? *Cleave* means "to cling to, to keep close." God wants the man to leave behind his parents and cling to his wife. Man and woman's most important relationship is with God. But after their relationship with

God, their marriage is to be the most important relationship they have.

Once the man leaves his family and cleaves to his wife, they are to become one flesh. They are to have a very special physical relationship that is only shared as a husband and a wife.

Let's read Genesis 1:28.

WHAT command did God give Adam and Eve when He blessed them?

____

____

God told Adam and Eve to have children and fill the earth and to rule over it. But in Genesis 3 we see the fall of man. Sin changes everything—even God's ideal plan for Adam and Eve.

Turn to Genesis 3:16 on page 194, and look at what God says to Eve.

HOW will Eve bring forth her children?

____

WHO is to rule over whom?

____

Now that sin has entered the world, we see that God has placed the husband to rule over the wife. WHAT does that mean? Let's check a cross-reference to see what God says about the marriage relationship in Ephesians 5. Look up and read Ephesians 5:22-32.

Ephesians 5:22-24 WHAT is the wife to do?

____

HOW is she to do this?

____

What does it mean "to be subject to"? That means to rank under. The wife is to respect her husband and to voluntarily put herself under her husband's authority, just like she would do in her relationship with Jesus.

Ephesians 5:25 HOW is the husband to treat his wife?

____

Look at Ephesians 5:28. HOW is the husband to love his wife?

____

Isn't that awesome? God compares the husband's relationship to his wife to that of Jesus and the church. When God talks about the church, He is talking about those who believe in Jesus and have surrendered their life to Him. We know that Jesus willingly gave up His life for the church. The husband is to give himself for his wife in the same way that Jesus did. He is to be unselfish and cherish her like he does his own body. He is to take care of her.

Do you see what a special relationship marriage is? Does God's plan for marriage sound like it is a temporary or permanent relationship? Look up and read Matthew 19:4-9.

Matthew 19:6 WHAT does God say about the marriage relationship?

____

Try this: Take two pieces of construction paper and glue them together. After the glue has dried, try separating the two pieces of paper. Can you separate the pieces of paper cleanly, or does some of the paper tear off and stay stuck to the other piece of paper?

____

Trying this experiment will help you see that once two people have been joined as one, they cannot be separated without tearing and hurting each other. How do you think God feels about divorce since He created this special "one flesh" relationship? Look up and read Malachi 2:16.

HOW does God feel about divorce?

____

Now look at Matthew 19:9. WHAT is the only reason that Jesus gives for a divorce?

____

WHAT is immorality? That is when a person uses his or her body in a way that God says is wrong. It is the opposite of keeping your body pure.

Look at Hebrews 13:4. HOW is marriage to be held?

____

WHAT is the marriage bed to be?

____

Undefiled means to be pure. That means the marriage bed is only for the husband and wife's special relationship. It is not to be shared with anyone before you are married or with anyone after you are married, except the one you are married to. It is a special relationship that God has created for marriage only. Breaking that special relationship by being impure is the only reason that God gives for divorce.

Now that you have taken a closer look at marriage, do you see how serious marriage is to God? ___ Yes ___ No

God created marriage, and our marriage should glorify Him. By taking a closer look at the most important relationship we will ever have outside of our relationship with God, we can make sure that we do things His way and not follow what the world says is okay.

Do you remember how God brought the woman to the man? It is never too early for you to pray and ask God if it is His plan for you to marry, and for Him to bring the right person to you. Marriage is a lifetime commitment. We need to let God choose that special person to share our lives with.

As you grow up, ask God if you should date, and whom you should date. Choose the people you date very carefully. Don't let your feelings and emotions take over. Don't date someone because he or she is "cool" or popular. Ask yourself: Does this person love Jesus and live for Him? What is this person's character like? How does he/she treat his/her parents, brothers, and sisters?

Remember, we are to keep ourselves pure for our mate, so we need to watch how we behave. Should you be kissing and touching? God has told us that there is only one person that we should have this special relationship with: the person we are married to.

Don't do what everyone else says is okay. Do what God says is right. God tells us in 1 Corinthians 6:19-20 that our body is a temple of the Holy Spirit and does not belong to ourselves. We have been bought with a price. Jesus died for us on a cross; therefore, we are to give God glory with the way we use our bodies.

When you become a teenager, you may want to do a deeper study on marriage. We have a special Bible study called *Someday, a Marriage Without Regrets* that will prepare you for that very special relationship that God created.

Now as we head back to our campsite, did you learn your memory verse this week? Don't forget to say it to a friend or a grown-up.

4

A Big Find!

Genesis 4–5

Doesn't it feel good to be back at the campsite? We had quite a scary adventure last week as we searched for Max and rushed him to the hospital. Now that he is well and back at the campsite, we need to get back to work at the pit to find out what happened to Adam and Eve after God sent them out of the garden. But before we get started digging, let's have breakfast with the dig team.

Scraping Away the Dirt

As Uncle Jake walked up to the campfire to grab a cup of coffee, he noticed a very quiet and sad-looking Max. "Hey, Max, how are you feeling this morning?"

"I'm okay, Uncle Jake. Still sore from the sting, but that's all."

"Are you sure, Max? Or is something bothering you?"

"I just feel so bad, Uncle Jake. I know I let you down, and I hurt a lot of other people, too. I scared Molly, and Mary Frances almost got hurt trying to rescue me," finished Max.

"Well, Max, sin doesn't just affect you. It affects other people, too. Have you gone to God and told Him you are sorry and you don't want it to happen again?"

"Yes, sir, I did."

"What does God tell us He will do when we confess our sin?"

"He will forgive us."

"That's right. God has forgiven you, Max. Now you need to make things right with the people you hurt. You need to go to the dig team and to Molly, and you need to call your mom and dad."

"But didn't you call Mom and Dad, Uncle Jake?"

"Yes, I did. But I called them about your accident. You need to talk to them about what you did."

"I know," sighed Max. "What if Mom and Dad want me to come home early? Will Aunt Kathy and Uncle Kyle let Molly stay?"

"I don't know, Max. We'll just have to wait and see, okay? Right now we need to discuss your discipline for disobeying me. I love you, buddy, but you won't be allowed to help at the dig site for one week. Instead, you will work with Mr. Jim doing kitchen duty and also cleaning up at the site. Okay?"

"But, Uncle Jake..." Max started to protest, but instead he swallowed his protests and changed his response. "Yes, sir," he replied. "I'm really sorry."

"And I forgive you. Now," Uncle Jake smiled and placed his arm around Max's shoulders, "let's go pray with the team, and then you can call your mom."

How about you, junior archaeologists—have you prayed?

Then let's head over to the dig site and help Molly and the team uncover what happened after Adam and Eve were sent from the garden.

Turn to page 195 of your Observation Worksheets and read Genesis 4. Then mark the following key words and any pronouns or synonyms that go with these words with a special color or symbol:

Lord (God) (draw a purple triangle and color it yellow)

Adam (draw an orange)   Cain (draw a green)

Abel (draw a dark-blue)   Seth (draw a light blue)

death, kill, slay (draw a black tombstone and color it brown)

offering (box it in blue and color it yellow)

blood (draw in red)   sin (color it brown)

Now pull out your daily journal and make a list of everything you have discovered about Cain and Abel.

Daily Journal on Cain and Abel	
Cain	**Abel**

Wow! Look at all you have discovered, and that's not all. Scrape off a little more dirt on the right side of your square. Why, that looks like part of an old stone wall! As you continue to scrape away the dirt, why don't you uncover this week's memory verse? Unscramble the mixed-up words on the exposed stone wall below, and place the correct words in the blanks below to complete your memory verse.

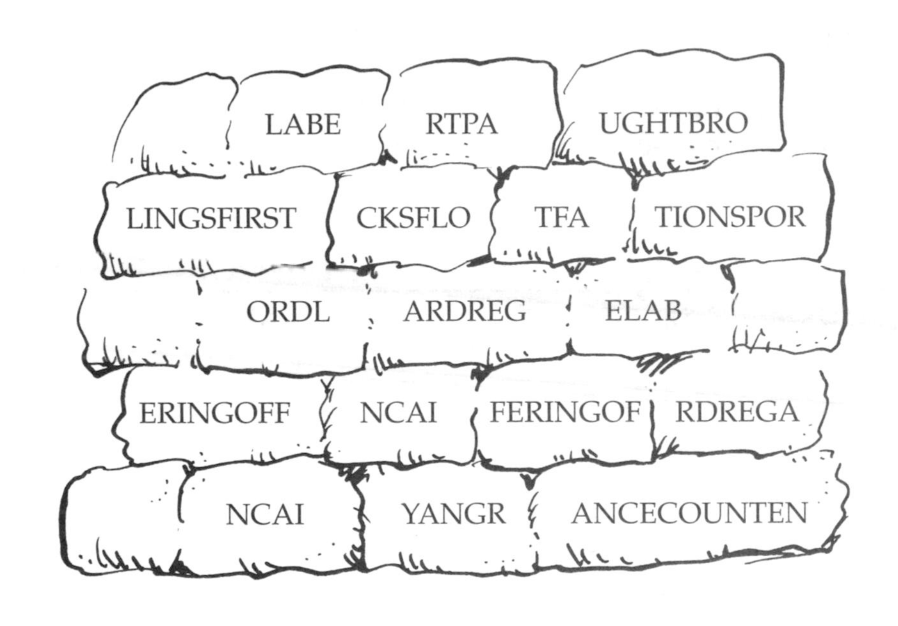

__________, on his __________ also ____________ of the

________________ of his _____________ and of their _________

______________. And the ____________ had ____________ for

_________ and for his _______________; but for ___________

and for his ________________ He had no _______________. So

___________ became very _____________ and his

________________ fell.

Genesis 4: _____ - _____

Now write this out on an index card and practice it how many times today? ____ times

DIGGING AND SIFTING

That was a neat discovery you made yesterday. The whole dig team is so excited that they can't wait to get back to the pit this morning to see how much of that old wall is still intact. Max was looking pretty disappointed as Molly headed for the site and he was left behind to clean up the dishes. Why don't you head over to the pit? We have a lot more to discover about Cain and Abel.

Now as you climb back into the pit, answer the 5 W's and an H.

In Genesis 1:28, God told Adam and Eve to be fruitful, multiply, and fill the earth. Now look at Genesis 4:1-2 on page 195.

WHOM did Eve give birth to?

____

Genesis 4:2 WHAT was Abel's job?

____

WHAT was Cain's job?

____

Genesis 4:3-4 WHAT did Cain and Abel do?

____

Genesis 4:3 WHAT was Cain's offering?

____

Genesis 4:4 WHAT was Abel's offering?

____

Genesis 4:4-5 WHAT was God's response?

____

WHY do you think God liked Abel's offering and not Cain's?

____

Did God like Abel better than Cain? ___ Yes ___ No

No way! God doesn't choose favorites. So WHY did God reject Cain's offering? Let's find out. Look up and read Hebrews 11:1-6.

Hebrews 11:2 HOW did the men of old gain approval?

____

Hebrews 11:4 WHAT does this tell us about Abel's and Cain's sacrifices?

____

HOW did Abel offer a better sacrifice than Cain?

____

WHAT testimony did Abel obtain by his sacrifice? That he was ______________________

Hebrews 11:6 WHAT is the only way we can please God?

____

Look up and read Romans 10:17.

HOW does faith come?

____

Now let's sift through the soil. We see that God accepted Abel's sacrifice because it was a better sacrifice. WHAT made it a better sacrifice? Abel's sacrifice was better because it was offered by WHAT? By f __ __ __ __

And faith comes by WHAT? By h __ __ __ __ __ __

Faith is the only way to please God. Abel understood this and brought God an offering in order to please Him. Either Cain didn't understand or he didn't care because he came to

God his way, by his works. Cain brought God an offering that came from what he had done with his own hands.

But didn't Abel offer God something from his works since he was a keeper of flocks? What is the difference in the two sacrifices? Remember, Hebrews said Abel's was offered by faith. Abel offered the sacrifice God wanted him to offer.

But HOW did Cain and Abel know what kind of offering to bring God? Do you remember what we saw last week in Genesis 3:21?

WHAT did God sacrifice in order to cover Adam and Eve's sin?

____

Cain and Abel had a picture of sacrifice from what God did in the garden to cover Adam and Eve.

Do you think that people today try to come to God their own way like Cain did? ___ Yes ___ No

Yes. A lot of people don't think it matters what you believe or how you come to God. Did it matter to God that Cain didn't offer the right sacrifice? It sure did! God wants us to have a relationship with Him, but we have to come to Him His way. We cannot earn our salvation by the work of our hands like Cain tried to do.

Look up and read Ephesians 2:8-9.

HOW are you saved?

____

WHAT is salvation?
It is the _____________ of God; not as a result of _____________, so that no one may _____________.

Look up and read John 14:6.

WHAT is the only way you can come to the Father?

____

God tells us very clearly in His Word that there is only one way to Him, and that is through His one and only Son, Jesus Christ, who shed His blood for our sin. Salvation is God's gift. If we don't come to God in faith and accept His Son as Savior of our life, then we will be rejected just like Cain's offering was rejected.

> Looking at all you have uncovered today, have you ever come to God His way? Or are you still trying to come to God the way you think is best?
>
> ____

As we have discovered, doing things our way only leads to sin and death.

Now take a look at how much of the old rock wall you uncovered today. Let's practice our memory verse as we help Mary Frances take pictures of the wall. Tomorrow we'll continue to scrape away the dirt and take a closer look at what happens after God rejects Cain's offering.

EXPOSING THE WALL

"Wow, that old stone wall is so cool," Max told Molly as he peered down into the pit. "I wish I could go down there and help with the excavation."

"I know, Max. It's not as much fun without you," Molly sighed. "But Uncle Jake thinks we will probably uncover more walls as we continue to dig."

"I sure hope so." Max checked his watch. "I better head back to the cook tent and finish helping Mr. Jim."

"Okay, Max. I'll go grab my gear and meet you at the campfire for breakfast."

Now that you have finished breakfast, junior archaeologists, are you ready to head back to Genesis 4? Turn to page 195 and read Genesis 4:3-16.

Genesis 4:5 WHAT happened to Cain when God rejected his offering?

____

Genesis 4:6 WHAT did God ask Cain?

____

Countenance means "face." Cain's face showed how he felt on the inside.

Genesis 4:7 Does God give Cain another chance?
___ Yes ___ No

Genesis 4:7 WHAT does God tell Cain?
"If you _______ _______, will not your countenance be ___________ ______? And if you do not ______ ______ , _________ is __________________ at the door; and its _____________ is for you, but you must master it."

Did you notice that Cain never asked God why He didn't accept his offering? Cain knew why. Cain never says, "I'm sorry I made a mistake. I did the wrong thing," even though God gives him the opportunity to confess by asking him in verse 6 why he is angry.

We see by God's response to Cain, "if you do well..." that Cain knew the right thing to do. Then God gives Cain another chance by giving him a choice to do well or to not do well. He had a choice to obey God and do what God had told him to do, or to do it his way.

God also warns Cain that if he doesn't do well, that sin is going to take over and master him. So WHAT does Cain choose: his way or God's, to master sin or to let sin overtake him? Let's find out.

Genesis 4:8 WHAT did Cain do?

____

Did Cain let his anger rule? ___ Yes ___ No

Let's read Ephesians 4:26-27. HOW are we to handle anger?

____

Did Cain give the devil an opportunity by being angry?
___ Yes ___ No

Did sin overtake Cain? ___ Yes ___ No

Did Cain obey God? ___ Yes ___ No

Genesis 4:9 WHAT did God ask Cain?

____

Did God know what had happened to Abel?
___ Yes ___ No

So if God knew, then WHY do you think He asked Cain this question?

____

HOW did Cain respond to God's question?

____

Did Cain confess to God what he had done, or did he lie?

____

Genesis 4:10 WHAT did God say?

____

Genesis 4:11-12 WHAT did God do to Cain?

____

Genesis 4:13-14 HOW did Cain respond?

____

Did Cain ever confess, did he ask for forgiveness, or was he only concerned about his punishment?

____

Genesis 4:15 WHAT did God do?

____

Was God merciful to Cain? ___ Yes ___ No

Genesis 4:16 WHAT did Cain do?

____

WHERE does Cain settle?

____

Let's look at a cross-reference that tells us about Cain. Look up and read 1 John 3:11-12.

1 John 3:11 HOW are we to treat one another?

____

1 John 3:12 Did Cain love his brother? ___ Yes ___ No

WHY did Cain kill his brother?

____

Now let's apply all that we have learned about Cain to our life.

HOW do you behave when you get angry?

Do you slam doors? Do you lash out by being sarcastic? Do you yell at the person who made you mad? Do you talk about them behind their back? Do you pout? Do you let your anger rule?

Write out how you act when something or someone makes you mad.

____

____

HOW should you behave? Look at Ephesians 4:26,31-32.

WHAT does God tell us to do with anger?

Be ___________, and yet do not ____________;

do not let the _______ ______ _________ on your anger.

P__ __ it a __ __ ___ from you.

Be _________ to _______ ________________.

F___ ___ ___ ___ ___ ___ each other, just as God in Christ also has forgiven you.

Do you have to have your way? ___ Yes ___ No

Do you love others? ___ Yes ___ No

Do you make fun of other kids, laugh at them, or talk mean about them? ___ Yes ___ No WHO are you behaving like? ______________

Do you only care about yourself and what you want? ___ Yes ___ No

Do you get jealous or angry when someone gets something that you want? ___ Yes ___ No

Are you walking God's way, or in the way of Cain?

____

Isn't it heartbreaking to see that Cain went out from the presence of the Lord? Can you imagine how awful it would be to not have God's presence in your life? But that is exactly what happens to us when we choose our way over God's way. As we climb out of the pit, brush off the dirt and ask God to help you always choose His way and not the way of Cain.

CLEARING AWAY THE RUBBLE

Good morning! That old stone wall is coming along. It takes a lot of patience to gently scrape away the dirt, keeping the wall intact, and you are doing a terrific job. Today we need to clear away some of the rubble to see what happens now that Cain has left God's presence and settled in the land of Nod.

Read Genesis 4:16-25 on page 197 of your Observation Worksheets.

Genesis 4:16-17 WHAT do we learn about Cain?

He has a w __ __ __.

He has a s __ __ named ____________.

He builds a ____________ and names it ____________.

So WHERE did Cain get his wife? Do you know?

Read Genesis 3:20. WHY did Adam call his wife Eve?

____

Read Genesis 5:4. Did Adam and Eve have other children? ___ Yes ___ No

Now let's look at the facts. Adam and Eve are the only people that God created. Eve is the mother of all the living. Adam and Eve had other children. So WHOM did Cain marry?

____

Now, the Bible does teach that we aren't to marry blood relatives because it can cause genetic problems, but God doesn't give this law until much later in the history of mankind. Right now we are at the beginning of mankind.

Let's do a family tree on all of Cain's descendants by reading Genesis 4:17-24 and filling out Cain's side of the family tree on the next page.

Since we are talking about the beginning of mankind, have you ever seen cavemen on TV, in books, or in movies? HOW are they portrayed: as very smart people, or as very primitive people who can't talk, write, or make things?

____

HOW do we know what the early people were really like? Let's take a look at Genesis 4:17-22 to see what God has to say about the first civilization.

Genesis 4:17 WHAT did Cain build? ________________

Genesis 4:20 WHERE did Jabal's children live?

____

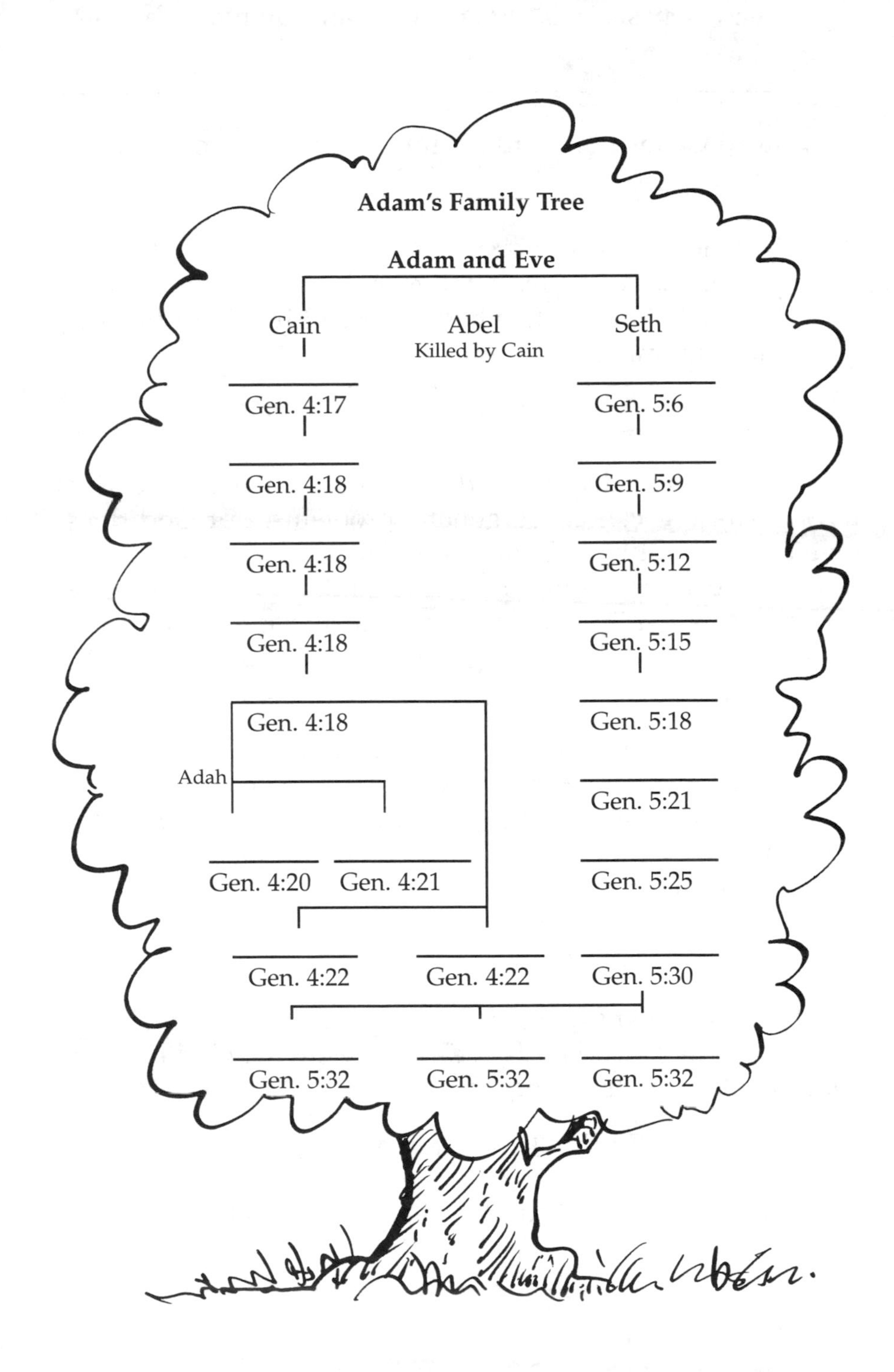
Adam's Family Tree
Adam and Eve
Cain
Abel
Killed by Cain
Seth
Gen. 4:17
Gen. 5:6
Gen. 4:18
Gen. 5:9
Gen. 4:18
Gen. 5:12
Gen. 4:18
Gen. 5:15
Gen. 4:18
Gen. 5:18
Adah
Gen. 5:21
Gen. 4:20
Gen. 4:21
Gen. 5:25
Gen. 4:22
Gen. 4:22
Gen. 5:30
Gen. 5:32
Gen. 5:32
Gen. 5:32

WHAT did they have?

____

Genesis 4:21 WHAT did Jubal's children do?

____

Genesis 4:22 WHAT did Tubal-cain do?

____

Amazing! The very first people were smart enough to build cities. They lived in tents, raised livestock, played musical instruments, and made tools of bronze and iron. Does that sound like the cavemen you have seen on TV or in books? No way! Man did not evolve and get smarter as time went by and he learned more. God created man, and he had both skills and intelligence.

Does this show you how dangerous it is to get your ideas of what man was like from the world? We need to always check out what man teaches us to see if it lines up with what God tells us in the Bible. We know that the Bible is pure truth. It is God's Word, and we are to take God at His Word no matter what man may tell us. We need to know WHOM we are going to believe: God or man.

MEASURING OUR FIND

Whew, it's hot today! Let's go ask Max for some lemonade to drink as we head back to the pit. Now that we have finished exposing our stone wall, we need to measure it and record our findings in our journal. So grab those tape measures and turn to page 198. Let's read Genesis 4:25-26.

Genesis 4:25 WHAT did Eve do?

____

Genesis 4:26 WHO was Seth's son?

____

WHAT happened after Seth had his son?

____

As we wrap up Genesis 4, we can see there is a contrast between Cain and his descendants and Seth and his descendants.

To find the contrast, take a look at Genesis 4:16.

WHAT did Cain do?
Went out from the ______________________________

Genesis 4:23 Cain's descendant Lamech followed in Cain's footsteps. WHAT did he do?

____

Now look at Seth's descendants again.
Genesis 4:26 WHOM did they call on?

____

Do you see the contrast—the difference in Cain's descendants' relationship with God and Seth's descendants' relationship with God?

Genesis 4:16 Cain w __ __ __ o __ __ from the
________________ of the Lord.

But

After Seth's son Enosh was born, then men began to c __ __ __ u __ __ __ the __ __ __ __ of the Lord.

Now read Genesis 5:1-32 and mark the following key words and the key phrase below, along with any pronouns and synonyms that go with them. A key phrase is like a key word, except it is a group of words that are repeated instead of just one word, such as "I did it." The group of words "I did it" is a phrase that is repeated instead of just one word.

Adam (draw an orange) Seth (draw a light blue)

likeness (image) (color it purple)

"and he died" (key phrase—underline it in brown)

Genesis 5:1 WHOSE likeness was man (Adam) created in?

____

Genesis 5:3 WHOSE image and likeness was Seth created in?

____

WHAT happened to all these men in chapter 5 except Enoch?

____

Genesis 5:23-24 WHAT happened to Enoch?

____

Now let's turn to page 198 and fill in Seth's side of the family tree by looking at Genesis 5:3-32 and listing his descendants on the tree on page 90.

Wow! Look at what you have uncovered in the first five chapters of Genesis: the creation of the world, the first marriage, the first sin, the first murder, the first civilization, and the first genealogy. You have done a super job.

Before you head to the campfire for the sing-along, why don't you make a family tree of your family? Ask your mom or dad to help you.

THINGS YOU'LL NEED

Construction paper or scrapbooking paper
Copies of family photos
Pens or markers
Glue and scissors

After you have all your supplies, draw a family tree on your paper. Start with the name of the oldest relative that your parents can remember, and then begin listing their descendants. You can use the family tree that we did on Cain and Seth as your guide. Make sure that you leave a place above their name for any pictures that you have of your descendants. If you don't have pictures of some of your family members, then just list their names. If you do have pictures, then glue their pictures above their names.

As you work on your project, ask your mom and dad to tell you something that they know about your descendants. Were they farmers, doctors, or homemakers? Where were they born? Do your parents know any stories about their lives? Did they know Jesus? Did they live godly lives? Then once you are finished, you will have a history of your family that you can share with your friends and with your children one day.

5

GENESIS 5–6

Last week as we discovered our old stone wall, we saw that after Adam and Eve left the garden, they began to have children. Their firstborn, Cain, chose to do things his way. He murdered his brother, Abel, and turned away from God. Another son, Seth, had a son named Enosh, and men began to call on God.

So WHO are those men that called on God? As we continue our expedition, we want to take a closer look at two of Seth's descendants who called on God—WHO they were, WHAT they were like, and WHAT the earth was like in their time.

MAPS AND COMPASSES

"Hey, Molly," Max called out. "Hurry up. I can't wait to go see Uncle Jake."

"I'm coming, Max. I just can't find my shoe. I know I put both of my shoes right by my bed. You don't think Sam dragged it off, do you?"

"How can you say that? Look at that face," Max asked. "Is that the face of a shoe thief?"

"Hmmm," Molly said as she bent down to examine Sam's face. Sam leaped up, taking full advantage of the moment to catch Molly by surprise and give her face a good licking. "Oh yuck, Sam. Stop!" Molly laughed as Sam knocked her down. "Make him stop, Max!"

Laughing, Max started tugging on Sam's leash. "Okay, boy, that's enough. You really got her this time. Now, Molly, promise Sam you won't say anything else bad about him."

"I promise, I promise," giggled Molly. "Now get him off."

As Max dragged off an excited Sam, he saw Molly's shoe behind the tent flap. "There's your shoe, right behind the flap."

"Hey, guys." Uncle Jake met them at the tent opening. Max, let's talk about your restriction. Mr. Jim said that you worked really hard last week, and that you did everything he asked without a complaint. I am so proud of you! Now that your restriction is over, are you ready for a new adventure?"

"Oh, no!" exclaimed Max. "Not another adventure. That's what got me into trouble last time."

Molly and Uncle Jake both laughed at Max. "Max, it wasn't the adventure that got you in trouble. It was yourself."

"I know, Uncle Jake," laughed Max. "I'm ready. How about you, Sam?" Sam yapped and started wagging his tail.

"Okay, guys, then let's get moving. We need to meet Allie at the campfire."

How about you, junior archaeologists? Are you ready for a new adventure now that Max is back in action? Since Uncle Jake has everything running smoothly at the campsite, he is going to take us with him as he scouts future locations. Doesn't that sound like fun? Allie is going to be our guide, but before we get started we need to ask our "site boss" to guide us in our new adventure, as well as keep us safe.

Pray and then turn to page 198 and read Genesis 5. Last week we made a family tree of Adam's descendants through Seth.

Now go back to where you marked the key phrase "and he died" on your Observation Worksheets and write out beside it HOW old that person was when he died.

WHAT is unusual about these men?

____

Did you figure it out? These men all lived a really long time before they died. And HOW old were they when they had their children? Were they young, in their 20s or 30s, or were they older?

____

WHO lived the longest? ______________________

Genesis 5:22 WHAT did Enoch do after he had Methuselah?

Enoch ________ with ________ for ________ years.

Genesis 5:24 WHAT happened to Enoch?

____

WHAT does that mean? Read Hebrews 11:5.

Did Enoch die? ___ Yes ___ No

WHY not?

____

Isn't that awesome? Look at Jude 14-15. (Did you know that Jude has only one chapter? That's why you don't see a chapter number before the verse in Jude!)

WHAT did Enoch do?

____

WHAT did he prophesy? WHAT did he warn the people about?

____

Now let's make a list in our field notebook of what we have discovered about Enoch.

Enoch:
Genesis 5:24 Enoch ____________ with ___________.

Hebrews 11:5 By ____________ Enoch was __________ up so that he would not see _________________.

Hebrews 11:5 Enoch was ___________________ to God.

Jude 14-15 Enoch _____________ judgment upon all, to _____________ all the _____________ of all their _____________ deeds.

Seth's genealogy in Genesis 5 shows us a very special man, Enoch. We know that Enoch walked with God. We know he warned the ungodly men of God's coming judgment. And we know that by faith Enoch pleased God so much that God did not let him see death. Instead, God took him up to heaven without his ever dying. Unbelievable!

Now ask yourself, "Am I an Enoch?" One way we walk with God is to study His Word, which is what you are doing right now. We are so proud of you, and so is God!

So do you walk with God? ___ Yes ___ No

Do you believe God? That means to take Him at His Word. Do you do what God tells you to do? ___ Yes ___ No

Do you please God? Name one way you please God.

____

All right! Now before we head to the Jeep to scout locations with Uncle Jake and Allie, we need to grab our compasses. Let's practice using your compass to decode our memory verse for the week. The first blank of each word has a number under the blank. Find the number on your compass, and place the letter that is in the box with the number on the first blank in the word. Using that first letter as a starting point, follow the compass directions under the other blanks in the word to find the rest of the letters for that word. N=north or up, S=south or down, E=east or right, W=west or left. NW, SW, SE, NE are on the diagonals. The first word is done for you.

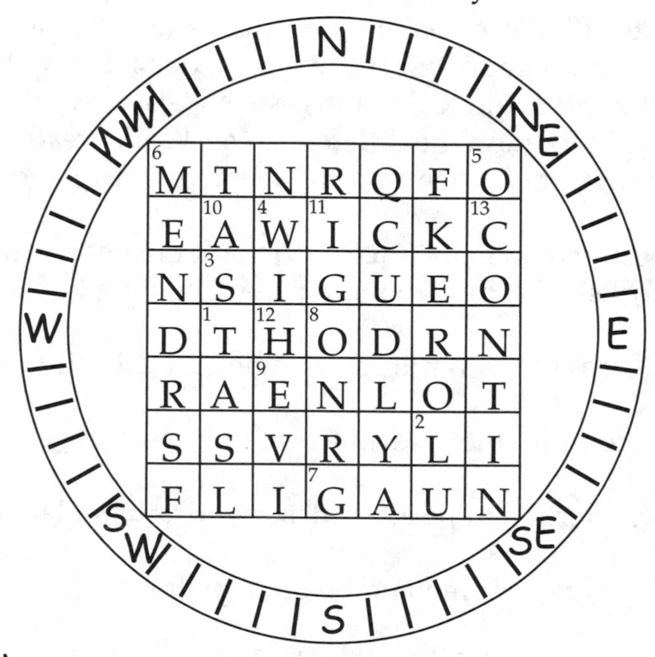

THEN ___ ___ ___ ___ ___

1 E S E 1 E S 2 N N W 3 N E 1 E SW N

___ ___ ___

1 E S 4 E E E S SW SW W SW W 5 W

___ ___ ___ ___ ___

6 SE SW 4 W S 7 N NW W N 8 S 1 E S

___, ___ ___ ___

9 W W NE E 10 SW S 1 E SW N 9 S N SE E

___ ___ ___

11 NW W SW S SE 5 W 1 E S

___ ___ ___

1 E E NE W SW W N 5 W 12 N W

___ ___ ___ ___

12 S W W NE 4 W S 8 S E S 9 S S W

___.

13 S S S S S W W NE NW S Genesis 6:_____

THE ADVENTURE BEGINS

We are off! We have our compasses and maps. Mr. Jim packed our food supplies, and we have our flashlights, ropes, tents, and our first aid kit, just in case. We also have the camera so we can photograph the different areas. We are ready to begin our adventure. Let's pile into the Jeep. Turn to page 201 and read Genesis 6.

The best way to get started is to mark our map (our Observation Worksheets) by looking for the following key words:

Lord (God) (draw a purple triangle and color it yellow)

Noah (color it blue) earth (color it brown)

flesh (underline in pink) destroy (draw in black)

covenant (color it red and box it in yellow)

God commanded (underline three times)

Now that we've marked our map, let's make a list about Noah in our field notebook on the next page.

FIELD NOTEBOOK

Noah:

Genesis 6:8 Noah __________ __________ in the ________ of the _________.

Genesis 6:9 Noah was a ________________ man.

Noah was ________________ in his time.

Noah ______________ with __________.

Genesis 6:10 Noah had ____________ __________ named __________, __________, and ____________.

Genesis 6:22 Noah did all that ________ had ______________.

Now compare Noah to Enoch. HOW are they alike?

____

Enoch and Noah walked with God and pleased Him. Why don't you please God by practicing your memory verse as we bounce along in the Jeep? Nothing pleases God more than for us to know His Word and have it hidden in our hearts.

FOLLOWING OUR MAP

Yesterday we marked our maps and discovered some very special things about Noah. We learned that Noah found favor with God. He was a righteous and blameless man who walked with God. Does that mean that Noah wasn't a sinner? No, it doesn't. Remember, once Adam and Eve sinned, then sin came into the world. We are all born sinners. Noah was righteous because he had a right relationship with God. Noah had put his faith in God and in the promise that God would send a redeemer to save him from his sins.

When we accept Jesus as our Savior, God sees us as righteous because, once we surrender our lives to Jesus, God sees Jesus' righteousness, not our sin. It gives us a right relationship with God.

Now let's take another look at Genesis 6 to see what the rest of the people on the earth were like in Noah's time.

Turn to page 201 of your Observation Worksheets on Genesis 6.

Make a list of everything you learn about the earth and God in your field notebook.

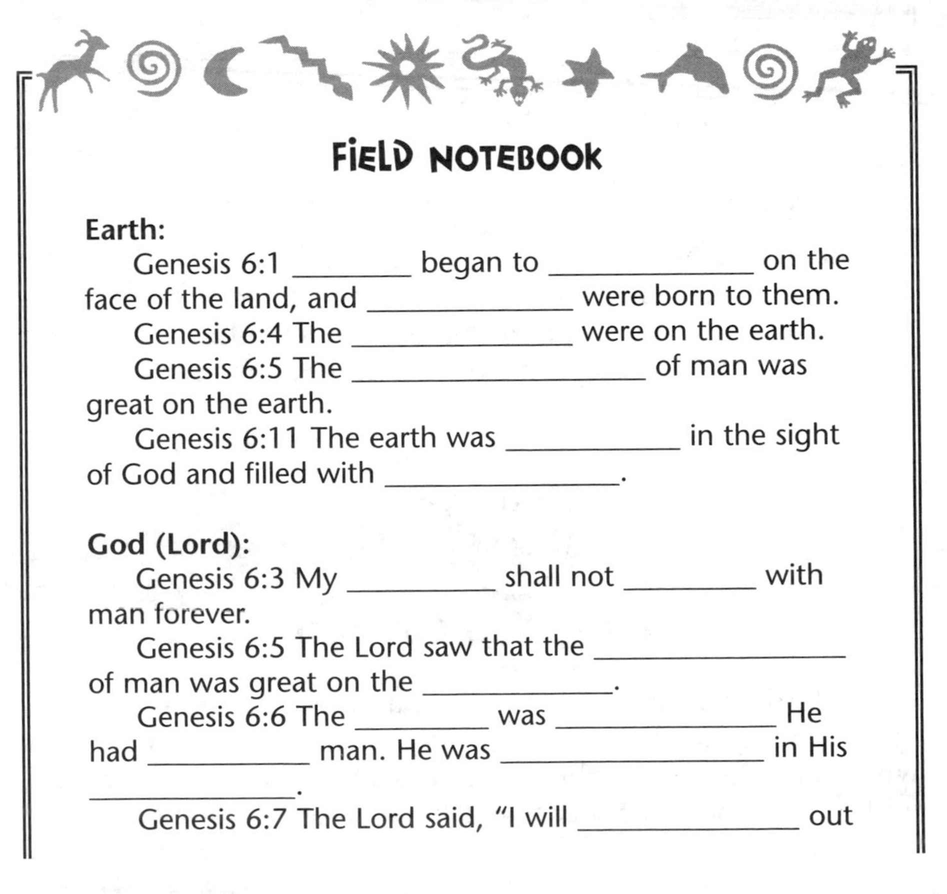

FIELD NOTEBOOK

Earth:

Genesis 6:1 ________ began to ______________ on the face of the land, and ______________ were born to them.

Genesis 6:4 The _______________ were on the earth.

Genesis 6:5 The ____________________ of man was great on the earth.

Genesis 6:11 The earth was ____________ in the sight of God and filled with ________________.

God (Lord):

Genesis 6:3 My __________ shall not _________ with man forever.

Genesis 6:5 The Lord saw that the _________________ of man was great on the _____________.

Genesis 6:6 The _________ was _______________ He had ___________ man. He was _________________ in His ______________.

Genesis 6:7 The Lord said, "I will _______________ out

__________ whom I have _______________ from the face of the land, from man to _______________ to _____________________________ and to _______________ of the sky; for I am _______________ that I have made them."

Genesis 6:13 I am about to _______________ them with the earth.

Genesis 6:17 I am bringing the _____________ of __________ upon the earth, to destroy all _____________.

Genesis 6:18 I will establish My _______________ with you.

Now find all the answers that you placed in the blanks on your lists and circle them in the word search below. Some answers may be used more than once, but you only need to circle them one time.

C	R	E	E	P	I	N	G	T	H	I	N	G	S
R	T	P	F	F	G	R	I	E	V	E	D	R	S
E	R	E	H	L	M	I	L	I	H	P	E	N	E
A	A	C	C	O	V	E	N	A	N	T	S	W	N
T	E	N	E	O	E	A	R	T	H	V	T	A	D
E	H	E	T	D	M	E	N	G	L	S	R	T	E
D	Y	L	P	I	T	L	U	M	P	F	O	E	K
A	B	O	U	S	L	A	M	I	N	A	Y	R	C
M	L	I	R	D	D	H	R	H	S	E	L	F	I
Y	O	V	R	M	B	I	R	D	S	E	D	N	W
Y	R	R	O	S	T	R	I	V	E	B	L	O	T
B	D	K	C	W	L	I	X	I	A	C	J	X	A

SCOUTING THE AREA

"Wow, Uncle Jake, look at those mountains," Molly cried out as the Jeep came to a stop in front of a small village.

"Oh, man, I sure would like to go mountain climbing," chimed in Max. "That would be so cool."

"Now, Max," winked Uncle Jake, "don't go getting any ideas."

Allie and Molly both laughed. "I won't," said Max. "But do you think we could take a small hike?"

"What do you think, Allie?" asked Uncle Jake.

"I've hiked in this area before, and it's pretty safe," Allie answered. "But we better get started scouting the area first. The place you wanted to look at is about a mile to the northwest."

"Great. Molly, how would you like to try out your compass skills and get us started in the right direction?"

"Yea!"

"Then, lead the way."

Do you have your compass ready, junior archaeologists? Point it northwest and turn to page 201. Our careful study of Genesis 6 yesterday has shown us that while Noah walked with God, the rest of the earth was filled with wickedness and violence. Let's read Genesis 6:1-22.

Genesis 6:3 WHAT is God going to do to man's days?

____

WHY?

____

Genesis 6:5 WHAT do we learn about man?

____

Genesis 6:6 HOW did God feel about man?

____

Genesis 6:7 WHAT is God going to do?

____

Did God feel the same way about Noah? Look at Genesis 6:8 to find your answer.

____

Genesis 6:12 WHAT do you see about the flesh and the earth?

____

Genesis 6:7,13 WHY is God going to destroy the earth?

____

____

Genesis 6:14 WHAT does God tell Noah to do?

____

Genesis 6:17 HOW will God destroy all flesh?

____

Genesis 6:18-22 Is God going to blot out Noah?
___ Yes ___ No

Genesis 6:18 WHAT is God going to do with Noah?

____

Genesis 6:18 WHO will enter the ark?

____

Genesis 6:9 WHY will Noah and his family escape the flood?

____

Genesis 6:18-21 WHAT is Noah to take on the ark?

____

____

Genesis 6:22 Did Noah obey God? ___ Yes ___ No

God is going to judge the world because of its wickedness. The earth and all the flesh on it are so corrupt that God is grieved and sorry that He made man—except for one man, Noah, and his family. Let's do some cross-referencing to find out more about Noah and what God's Word has to say about judgment.

Look up and read 2 Peter 2:5. WHAT is Noah?

____

Hebrews 11:7 HOW did Noah prepare an ark for salvation? By f __ __ __ __

Matthew 24:37-39 WHAT was happening in the days of Noah before the flood?

____

____

Does God warn us that He will send judgment? Look at Enoch. Enoch prophesied about the coming judgment before

God took him up. Look at Noah. He was a preacher of righteousness. He warned the people about the coming judgment of the flood. Now look at God's Word. Read 2 Peter 3:5-11.

Is God warning about a coming judgment?
___ Yes ___ No

2 Peter 3:9 Does God want people to perish?
___ Yes ___ No

WHAT is God's desire?

____

2 Peter 3:11 WHAT are you to be like?

____

God loves us. He wants us to repent and turn to Him. Those who repent (have a change of mind and therefore turn away from their sin and put their faith in Him) will be saved.

Did you know that there is another judgment coming? One day soon God will judge the earth again. The passage we just looked at in Matthew 24:37-39 and the passage in 2 Peter 3:5-11 are warning of the coming of the Son of Man (Jesus' second coming). The first time Jesus came to earth, it was to save us. The next time He comes, it will be as a judge. But those who belong to Him will be saved from that judgment just like Noah and his family were saved from the judgment of the flood.

HOW about you? Do you believe judgment is coming? Are you ready?

HOW would God describe you—blameless and righteous, or full of wickedness?

____

Are you living a life of faith like Noah?
___ Yes ___ No

Remember, God doesn't want anyone to perish. Live your life for Him, and share your faith with other people.

LOOKING FOR CLUES

"How am I doing, Uncle Jake?" Molly asked as she led the group toward an area of trees.

"Great. We are right on target. Max, can you tell me approximately how far we have walked?"

"I think we have gone about three quarters of a mile," answered Max as he checked his gauge.

"Good work. We only have a little farther to go. Why don't you two start looking around to see if there are any clues that would tell us whether people lived around here in the past?"

"All right! Come on, Sam. Start sniffing. Are you coming, Molly?"

"I'm right here," Molly laughed.

Let's get started. Studying Genesis 6 has shown us how much sin changed God's perfect world. The people became so wicked and full of violence that God was grieved and sorry that He made man. Now He is going to send a horrible judgment to destroy all flesh on the earth except for one righteous man and his family.

Today as we go back to Genesis 6 on page 203, let's take a look at God's instructions to Noah. Read Genesis 6:13-22 and make a list of all the instructions that God gave Noah in your field notebook.

FIELD NOTEBOOK

God's Instructions to Noah
Genesis 6:14 Make an ________________________

WHAT kind of wood? ________________________

HOW many rooms—one room or many rooms? _______

WHAT would make it waterproof?

____

Genesis 6:15 WHAT size was it to be?
HOW long? ________________________

HOW wide? ________________________

HOW tall? ________________________

Genesis 6:16 Did it have any windows? If so, HOW many and WHERE were they?

____

HOW about doors? ________________________

HOW many decks? ________________________

Genesis 6:18 WHO was to enter the ark?

____

Genesis 6:19-21 WHAT did God tell Noah to take in the ark?

____

Now become the site artist by reading God's instructions to Noah and drawing a picture of what the ark would look like in the box below.

Some people say that it wasn't possible for all those animals to fit on the ark, or that the ark would have turned over during the raging of the floodwaters. Let's take a look in our field notebook below at God's master plan.

FIELD NOTEBOOK

The Master's Plan

God told Noah to build the ark 300 hundred cubits long, 50 cubits wide, and 30 cubits high. A cubit is approximately 18 inches, which means the ark was approximately 450 feet long by 75 feet wide, and 45 feet high. It had 95,000 square feet of space inside.

Do you know how big that is? If you were to watch a train go by pulling boxcars, you would have to watch 520 boxcars go by to equal the size of the ark. It was about the size of one and a half football fields. And it was about as tall as a four-and-a-half-story building. The ark was probably designed like a box, instead of being curved like you see in books.

How many animals do you think would fit in 520 boxcars?

Did you notice God told Noah to bring two of every *kind?* A kind is like a dog, cat, bird, etc. God wanted Noah to bring a male and female dog, a male and female cat, etc. Not a male and female of every type of dog or cat, such as a poodle, a beagle, a cocker spaniel, etc.

The ark was so big that there was plenty of room for all of the animals, creeping things, and birds, even the dinosaurs! All of God's living things would only take up half of the ark's deck space. Now we need to add Noah, his family, the animals that were to be used for sacrifice, and food to the other half of the deck space. Would that fill up the other side of the ark? No way! There would be plenty of room left over.

A man named Peter Jansen who lived in Holland built a model of the ark using the proportions in the Bible. His model of the ark showed that the ark was seaworthy and almost impossible to turn over. The ark was built for floating (like a giant barge). It was also engineered in such a way that it could handle the giant waves of the flood.

Amazing! God, our Master Designer, designed the perfect boat to rescue His people from the storms of the flood.

Take another look at Genesis 6:22: *"Thus Noah did; according to all that God had commanded him, so he did."* God designed the perfect boat. He told Noah what to do, and WHAT happened? Noah obeyed. By faith Noah trusted God to know what was best for his life. He followed God's plan.

Do you trust God to know what is best for you? _______

Do you follow His plans, or do you insist on having your way? ______________________________

WHAT would have happened if God had given you the plans for the ark?

____

____

Be like Noah. Follow God's plan. He loves you and only wants to give you His very best!

Did you remember to say your memory verse this week to a friend or grown-up? Great! Let's head for the mountains. It's time to go hiking!

6

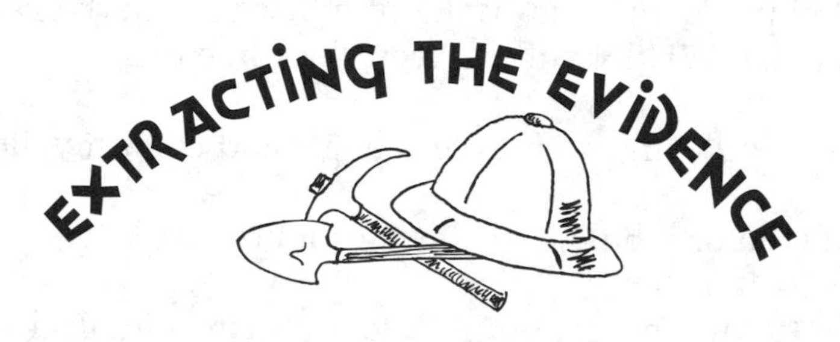

GENESIS 7

That was a great scouting expedition last week. Uncle Jake was able to get a lot of photos that will help him search for other dig sites. Now that we know God is going to judge the world with a flood, we need to head back to the pit and find out WHAT happens next. WHAT other instructions does God give? And HOW long will the flood last?

So grab those shovels and head back to the pit!

LET'S MARK OUR MAPS

"I loved hiking up those mountain trails. It was so cool!" Max told Molly as they headed to the pit.

"I know. It was so much fun. But I can't wait to get back into the pit with the dig team."

"Me, too, especially since I missed out on uncovering the wall. How about a race to the pit?" As soon as Max finished his question, he shouted, "Go!" and was off in a flash.

"Hey, no fair," yelled Molly as she took off after him.

After you race Molly and Max to the pit, turn to page 204 and read Genesis 7. We need to mark our maps by looking for the following key words. Make sure that you mark everything that tells you WHEN with a green clock like this:

Lord (God) (draw a purple triangle and color it yellow)

Noah (color it blue) earth (color it brown)

flesh (underline in pink) blot out (circle in black)

God commanded (underline three times) flood of water

all (color it green, box it in yellow) every (color it orange)

And the water prevailed (circle in red)

Now that you have Genesis 7 mapped out, let's uncover this week's memory verse by using our math skills. Don't you think Noah had to have good math skills to follow God's instructions for building the ark? Archaeologists need good math skills, too, so they can measure their site, know how far and how wide to dig, and to make sure their records are accurate.

So sharpen those math skills. Uncover your Bible verse by looking at the clues underneath the blanks below your research notes card. Each blank has a math problem underneath it. Work this problem and find the answer on your research notes card. Write the letter that goes with the correct answer on your card on the blank. For example, if the math problem is 5x7, look at your research notes card and find 35, the correct answer to the math problem 5x7. Then write the letter that goes with 35, which is the letter T, on the blank that has 5x7 underneath it.

Research Notes

A=6	B=8	C=10	D=12	E=14	F=16	G=18
H=9	I=15	J=21	K=24	L=27	M=20	N=28
O=36	P=44	Q=48	R=25	S=30	T=35	U=40
V=45	W=50	X=55	Y=60	Z=49		

Thus ____ ____ ____ ____ ____ ____ ____ ____ ____

3x3 7+7 2x4 30-3 6x6 7x5 30+5 2x7 6+6

____ ____ ____ ____ ____ ____ ____ ____

20+16 4x10 7x5 7+7 9x5 10+4 5x5 50+10

____ ____ ____ ____ ____ ____ ____ ____ ____ ____ ____

3x9 5x3 35+10 3x5 7x4 6x3 5x7 6+3 7+8 4x7 9+9

that was upon the ____ ____ ____ ____ of the land, from

8+8 3+3 2x5 8+6

____ ____ ____ to ____ ____ ____ ____ ____ ____ ____ to

10+10 4+2 4x7 3+3 30-2 5x3 10x2 5+1 3x9 5x6

____ ____ ____ ____ ____ ____ ____ ____

5+5 5x5 7+7 9+5 40+4 6+9 4x7 9+9

____ ____ ____ ____ ____ ____ and to

7x5 6+3 3x5 7x4 9+9 10+20

____ ____ ____ ____ ____ of the sky, and they were

4+4 3x5 5x5 4x3 6x5

____ ____ ____ ____ ____ ____ ____ ____ ____ ____ from

2x4 30-3 6x6 7x5 30+5 2x7 6+6 20+16 4x10 7x5

the ____ ____ ____ ____ ____; and only ____ ____ ____ ____

7+7 4+2 5x5 7x5 3x3 7x4 6x6 3+3 3+6

was left, together with ____ ____ ____ ____ ____ that were

40-5 10-1 6x6 5x6 9+5

with him in the ____ ____ ____.

7-1 5x5 6x4

Genesis 7: ____

Fantastic! Don't forget to write it out and say it aloud three times today. You are a mathematical whiz!

SIFTING THE SOIL

Good morning! Let's go meet Hannah, our soil scientist. Now that we have marked our maps, we need to sift the soil we dug up yesterday in the pit. We need to make sure that we don't miss any small finds as we continue to look at Genesis 7. Get your sifter from Hannah and turn to page 204 of your Observation Worksheets and read Genesis 7.

Last week as we looked at God's instructions to Noah, we saw that God told Noah to take his family; two of every living thing on the earth, a male and a female; and food for them to eat. Now let's look at the rest of the instructions that God gave Noah in Genesis 7.

Genesis 7:1 WHAT did God tell Noah to do?

____

Genesis 7:2 WHAT did God tell Noah to take with him?

____

HOW many clean animals?

____

HOW many unclean animals?

____

HOW many birds?

____

WHAT did God mean by "clean" and "unclean" animals? You have just uncovered a small find. Check out your research card below to find out what God means by "clean" and "unclean" animals.

"CLEAN" OR "UNCLEAN": WHAT'S THE DIFFERENCE?

WHY does God say that some animals are "clean" and others are "unclean"? Are some animals dirtier than others? No. God called the animals "clean" or "unclean" by the type of animal that they were.

So WHAT makes an animal "clean" or "unclean"?

"Clean" animals have a split hoof and chew cud.

"Unclean" animals do not chew cud, or do not have a split hoof.

WHY did it matter if an animal was "clean" or "unclean"?

God's people could only eat and sacrifice the animals that were "clean." Later on, after the flood, God gives the Jews the law explaining which animals are "clean" and which animals are "unclean."

To find out more about "clean" and "unclean" animals, you can also read Leviticus 11 and Deuteronomy 14.

Genesis 7:4 WHAT is God going to send?

____

Has it ever rained before on the earth? Take a look back at Genesis 2:5. ________________________________

So, had Noah ever seen it rain? ____________________

Yet he believed what God said. What faith! No wonder God called him a righteous man.

Genesis 7:4 WHEN does God tell Noah it is going to rain?

____

For HOW long? ________________________________

Genesis 7:4 WHAT is going to happen when God sends the rain?

____

So is this just an ordinary rain?

____

Do you know what that phrase *blot out* means? The Hebrew word for *blot out* is *machah*. It is pronounced maw-khaw, and it means "to wipe off, to be removed, to be effaced, to be destroyed."

Let's look at the Hebrew word for *flood*, *mabbul*, pronounced mab-bool'. It means "flood, deluge." Look up the word *deluge* in your dictionary. WHAT does it mean?

____

By looking at what these words mean, we can see that God is not sending an ordinary rain. God will send a great deluge that will overrun and overwhelm the earth with water. It will be a major catastrophe that will literally remove and destroy every living thing on the earth.

Genesis 7:8-9,15 HOW did all of the animals get into the ark? Did Noah and his family have to go out and round up two of every kind?

____

Genesis 7:16 WHAT happened after all flesh entered the ark as God commanded?

____

You make a great sifts-man! Now head back to camp to get rid of that extra dirt on your face. Oh, and don't forget Sam. He's rooting in his dirt pit. What a mess! He is one unclean animal!

RECONSTRUCTING THE SCENE

"Hey, Molly, hurry up," cried Max as he rushed into the tent. "Mr. Jim is going to let us help him cook breakfast over the open campfire this morning."

"Really, Max?" Molly jumped out of bed and ran over to her trunk. "It'll only take me a minute. Don't start without me; I'm coming." Molly's breathless words fell on top of each other as she raced around the tent trying to find her clothes and her gear.

"Ummm, Molly, are you sure you want to go outside looking like that?" Max laughed, as Molly came out from the dressing area. "Your shorts are inside out."

"Okay, wise guy," Molly huffed at Max, "just get out of the tent. I'll see you at the campfire."

So, junior archaeologists, are you "right side out" and ready to help cook the team's breakfast over an open fire? As we get started flipping pancakes and frying bacon (watch out for Sam), we need to head back to Genesis 7. But don't forget to talk to your "site boss" first.

Yesterday as we sifted through the soil, the last thing we saw was that God shut the door of the ark behind Noah. Today we need to reconstruct what happened. Look at your Observation Worksheets and find all the places you marked with a green clock to find out WHEN the rain begins, HOW long it lasts, and HOW old Noah is? Turn to page 204 and read Genesis 7.

Genesis 7:6 HOW old was Noah when the flood came?

____

Now think about this: Noah was a preacher who warned people about the coming flood, and we know that it had never rained on earth. Do you think the people teased Noah and made fun of him in the time it took him to build the ark?______________________

Did their teasing keep Noah from obeying God? ______

HOW about you? Do kids tease and make fun of you for believing in God, for reading your Bible, and for going to church? Do they tease you when you tell them you don't use bad words or watch bad movies?

____

Can the kids at your school see a difference in you?

____

Do you give in to their pressure and talk like them, wear clothes that they think are cool, and see movies you know are wrong, or do you stand firm like Noah did?

____

Now let's go back to the ark. Noah is 600 years old and God has shut the door.

Genesis 7:11 WHAT month and WHAT day does God send the flood? The ______________ month and the ______________ day

Genesis 7:12 HOW long did the rain fall?

____

HOW many months is that? ________________________

Genesis 7:24 HOW long did the water prevail upon the earth?

____

HOW many months is that? ________________________

Genesis 7:11 WHAT happened to start the flood?
All the ________________________ of the ____________

__________ ____________ open, and the
_____________________ of the ___________ were
opened.

Genesis 7:17-18 WHAT did the water do to the ark?

____

Genesis 7:19-20 WHAT did the water cover?

____

Genesis 7:21-22 WHAT happened to all flesh that moved on the earth?

____

Genesis 7:23 WHO survived?

____

God's judgment has fallen, and Noah is saved by his faith. Tomorrow we will take another look at verse 11 and HOW the flood happened. Now WHAT do you need to do before you make s'mores? Practice your verse so you have it down! And be careful with those s'mores—you don't want Sam getting yours. He loved your bacon at breakfast!

DIGGING DEEPER

Rise and shine! It's time to head back to the pit. What will we discover today? With all that digging, maybe we will come across another find soon.

Yesterday we looked at Genesis 7:11 and saw that the flood began by the fountains of the great deep bursting open and the opening of the floodgates of the sky. Now let's try to find out what that means. Take a look at Max and Molly's research card that shows exactly what these words mean in the Hebrew language.

Fountains: *ma 'yan,* pronounced mah-yawn', means "a spring"

Deep: *tehom,* pronounced teh-home', means "the deep, sea, abyss"

Burst open: *baqa',* pronounced baw-kah', means "to split, cleave, break open, divide, rip up, tear"

Floodgates: *'arubbah,* pronounced ar-oob-baw, means "window, chimney, floodgate"

Sky: *shamayim,* pronounced shaw-mah'-yim, means "aloft, the sky, height, heavens"

What an amazing sight that must have been—God ripping open the floor of the great deep (the seas), so that fountains like a spring would rush up out of the sea, while at the same time God opened a floodgate of water from the sky.

Have you ever seen Niagara Falls on TV or in a book? Can you imagine God sending down great sheets of rain from the sky like Niagara Falls?

Try drawing in the box below what you think it might have looked like when God burst open the great deep and opened the floodgates of the sky.

Did you know that some people don't believe there was a worldwide flood? They think that it was only a local flood.

WHAT did God say was covered in Genesis 7:19?

___

Did He say all of the mountains, or some of the mountains?

___

Let's do a cross-reference to see what other Scriptures say. Take another look at Matthew 24:38-39.

WHAT took them away?

___

Did it take some of them, or all of them? ___

Look up 2 Peter 3:3-7.

2 Peter 3:6 WHAT was destroyed by water? ___

When someone uses the word *world*, do you think of a city, a state, a country, or the whole world?

___

Did you know that hundreds of flood traditions have been passed down through the centuries? Nations from every continent have stories about a great flood. If the flood had been just a local flood, why would all of these different continents have stories about a great flood that happened?

Looking at our observations in Genesis and other passages of Scripture, do you think the flood was worldwide or only a local flood? ___

One reason that some people think the flood was a local flood instead of a worldwide flood is because they say if all the water was wrung out of the clouds it would only raise the sea level a half inch. They don't think there was enough water in the clouds to cause a worldwide flood. And they say if there was enough water, where did the water go after the flood?

Scientists who are Christians and believe what God's Word says have come up with different scientific models (ideas) on how the flood could have happened. One idea is that a meteorite could have hit the earth. Some scientists think there used to be a canopy of water over the earth and it collapsed. And another scientific model that was introduced in 1994 by three geologists—Steven Austin, Andrew Snelling, and Kurt Wise—along with three geophysicists—John Baumgardner, D. Russell Humphreys, and Larry Vardiman—explains that a worldwide flood could have happened by plate tectonics. WHAT is this scientific model called plate tectonics?

Let's find out. But before we look at this idea, we need to look at HOW God made the earth. The earth is made up of three layers: the core, the mantle, and the crust.

Get an apple and ask Mom or Dad to help you cut the apple in half. Cutting the apple in half will give you a model to help you see HOW the earth is made. Or you can make a model of the earth by using clay. Molly and Max's research card below will show you how to make a clay model.

THINGS YOU WILL NEED

three different colors of clay
a piece of thread about 2 feet in length

Make a small ball using one of your colors of clay.

Next take another color of clay and wrap it around your small ball to make a bigger ball. It should be a pretty thick layer.

Then take your last color of clay and wrap it around your ball. Make this layer a very thin layer.

Hold the thread tightly between both hands and slice through the middle of the clay ball in order to make two halves. Now you can see all three layers of your earth.

Let's look at the different layers of the earth.

WHAT part of the apple, or WHAT part of your clay model do you think represents the core of the earth? The core of the earth is like the core part of the apple, the part that is the deep center on your clay model. The core is deep in the center of the earth. It is divided into a solid inner core and a liquid outer core. It is about 21,000 miles from one side to the other and is probably as hot as 7200 degrees Fahrenheit. It is probably made of iron and nickel, and it is where we think the earth's magnetic field comes from.

The layer next to the core is the mantle. It is like the white part of the apple and is very thick. It is as hot as 3000 degrees Fahrenheit and is probably made of solid silicate rocks, which can behave like plastic under certain types of stress.

And the last layer of the earth is the crust. The crust is a very thin outer shell just like the skin on the apple. It is made up of two different types of rocks. The continental crust is made up of mostly granitic rocks, and the oceanic crust is made up of mostly basaltic rocks. The continental crust is less compact, so it is lighter and can float above the oceanic crust.

Now let's look at the idea called plate tectonics. As God burst open the great deep, these creationists think the ocean floor slid into the mantle very quickly, causing it to fill with the hot material from the mantle which would make it lighter. This lighter crust would push the ocean onto the continents (the dry land) and cause a global flood. Also, geysers of superheated gases (the fountains of the great deep) would result from the hot mantle coming up. These gases would condense and fall as an intense rain. Later, as the crust cooled back down and became heavier, the floodwaters would return to the oceans from off the earth.

All these ideas sound pretty amazing, don't they? But only God knows exactly how the flood happened. The most important thing we need to remember is that God's Word is pure truth, and we are to put our faith in Him and believe what His Word tells us, no matter how impossible it looks to us or to man.

We need to look at this awesome and cataclysmic event and see how mighty and awesome our God is. All power to control heaven and earth lies in His hands. As it says in Jeremiah 32:17,

> *Ah Lord GOD! Behold, You have made the heavens and the earth by Your great power and by Your outstretched arm! Nothing is too difficult for You.*

You made quite a discovery today! No matter how impossible man says a worldwide flood was, we know that it wasn't impossible because God is on His throne and nothing is too difficult for Him!

MORE RESEARCH

"What are you up to?" Uncle Jake asked Molly and Max as he approached the pit with Dr. Murphree and another person they hadn't seen before.

"We're scraping away some of this dirt very carefully," Molly answered, pushing her hair back. "We think we hit something, so we want to be careful."

"Good work," Uncle Jake responded. "I'll have William come over and take a look. Why don't you climb out of the pit for a few minutes? I have someone that I want you to meet."

"Okay, we'll be right there." Max and Molly laid down their trowels and climbed out of the pit.

"Molly, Max, this is Dr. Moses. She is a colleague of Dr. Murphree's from the university." Uncle Jake introduced Molly and Max to the lady standing next to Dr. Murphree. "She is a paleontologist. Do you know what she does?"

"She studies dinosaurs," exclaimed Max.

"That's right, I do," replied Dr. Moses. "Paleontologists study the fossil remains of plants and animals and try to figure out how these plants and animals lived, as well as how they came to be trapped and preserved by rocky minerals."

"We know how that happened," replied Molly. "We've been studying Genesis, and we know that God sent a great flood that trapped and preserved plants and animals."

"Wow," exclaimed Dr. Moses, "Dr. Murphree warned me that you guys were sharp. I'm impressed!"

"That's the reason I asked Dr. Murphree to bring Dr. Moses over to the site," Uncle Jake told Max and Molly. "I want you to learn about dinosaurs and other fossils while you are studying the flood."

"Man, that is so cool," Max cried out, "a real paleontologist teaching us about dinosaurs. When do we start?"

"How about you two getting cleaned up while I get Dr. Moses something to drink?" Uncle Jake replied. "You can meet Dr. Moses by the stream in about ten minutes."

"We'll be there," Molly chimed in. "Come on, Max. Let's race to the tent."

Now are you ready to learn about dinosaurs? People who believe in evolution say massive beasts died millions of years before man appeared on earth. Is that true? HOW old is the earth? In Genesis Part One we dug up the truth: The earth is not billions or millions of years old. It is only thousands of years old. And we also discovered what God created each day of Creation. So WHERE do dinosaurs fit in? WHEN did God create them? Did they go on the ark? HOW could a huge beast fit on the ark? Let's find out.

The word *dinosaur* is not used in the Bible. The first time the word *dinosaur* was used was in 1841 when Sir Richard Owen used it to describe some bones he had discovered. The word *dinosaur* means "terrible lizard," and technically the word refers only to land creatures.

Now we know why the Bible doesn't use the word *dinosaur*. It's because a man chose the word to fit a discovery that he made in 1841. But the Bible does describe some large and fearsome beasts. Let's take a look at what the Bible has to say about these beasts.

One of the words the Bible uses for large beasts is *tannin. Tannin* is a Hebrew word that is used 28 times in the Old Testament and is usually translated "dragon," especially in the King James Version. Modern translations sometimes translate this word differently, so it is hard to understand the original meaning of the word. Let's look at some examples in the Scriptures below. Mark the word in each passage below that you think describes the large beasts, the *tannin.*

> Genesis 1:21 *God created the great sea monsters and every living creature that moves, with which the waters swarmed after their kind, and every winged bird after its kind; and God saw that it was good.*

> Psalm 148:7 *Praise the LORD from the earth, sea monsters and all deeps.*

Isaiah 27:1 *In that day the LORD will punish Leviathan the fleeing serpent, with His fierce and great and mighty sword, even Leviathan the twisted serpent; and He will kill the dragon who [lives] in the sea.*

Looking at this last Scripture, Isaiah 27:1, not only do we see *tannin*, the dragon who lives in the sea, but another word is used for the great beasts. That word is *leviathan.* Go back to Isaiah 27:1 and mark every time you see the word *leviathan.* Now look at the Scriptures below and mark every reference to *leviathan.*

Psalm 104:26 *There the ships move along, and Leviathan, which You have formed to sport in it.*

Read all of Job 41 to see the entire description.

Job 41:1-2 *Can you draw out Leviathan with a fishhook? Or press down his tongue with a cord? Can you put a rope in his nose or pierce his jaw with a hook?*

Draw a picture of what you think a *tannin* and a *leviathan* would look like in the box below.

Now let's look at another word, *behemoth,* that is used once in Scripture in Job 40:15. The Hebrew word *behemoth* is a plural extension of the word *behemah,* a word that is used 137 times in the Old Testament to refer to four-footed animals. It is translated "cattle, animals, beasts," but when it is used as *behemoth,* it is referring to a brute beast.

Job is one of the more ancient books in the Bible and was probably written within a few centuries *after* the flood. It is also the only place the word *behemoth* is used. Mark every reference to *behemoth* and the pronouns that go with *behemoth* in the Scriptures below.

> Job 40:15-23 *Behold now, Behemoth, which I made as well as you; he eats grass like an ox. Behold now, his strength in his loins and his power in the muscles of his belly. He bends his tail like a cedar; the sinews of his thighs are knit together. His bones are tubes of bronze; his limbs are like bars of iron. He is the first of the ways of God; let his maker bring near his sword. Surely the mountains bring him food, and all the beasts of the field play there. Under the lotus plants he lies down, in the covert of the reeds and the marsh. The lotus plants cover him with shade; the willows of the brook surround him. If a river rages, he is not alarmed; he is confident, though the Jordan rushes to his mouth.*

Describe WHAT the *behemoth* looks like.

____

____

WHAT does the *behemoth* eat?

____

Is the *behemoth* strong? ___ Yes ___ No

Draw a picture of what you think a *behemoth* would look like in the box below.

So WHEN did God create dinosaurs? Look back at Genesis 1 if you need some help remembering and record WHAT day God created dinosaurs. ___________
Did dinosaurs go on the ark? Look at Genesis 6:19-20 and Genesis 7:14-15. ______________________________

Did you know that most dinosaurs were not any larger than a sheep? Some were no larger than a chicken. The largest dinosaur was probably no bigger than today's blue whale. Although the ark was large enough to take full-grown animals, it does not necessarily mean that God had Noah take the full-grown older animals on the ark. Noah could have taken baby or younger animals that would have been smaller.

So WHAT happened to the dinosaurs after the flood? HOW do we know that dinosaurs came off the ark? Did anyone ever see a dinosaur after the flood? Think about the Book of Job and what you learned about *behemoth*.

WHEN did Job live: before or after the flood?

____

Have you ever heard any dragon stories? _______________

Have you heard about anyone seeing this kind of creature today? WHAT about people that claim to have seen a sea monster in a lake in Scotland?

Could there still be a few around today?______________

WHY do you think that?

____

____

So WHAT happened to the dinosaurs? Have you learned about animals in school that are endangered? How about animals that have become extinct (that means they are no longer alive)? Over a period of time many animals have become endangered to where there are only a few left that are still alive today. While a lot of other animals have become extinct, dinosaurs have completely died out. We don't know for sure if the dinosaurs are extinct, or if there are still a few around today since there have been sightings of dinosaur-like creatures. But we do know WHO made them, as well as all the other fantastic creatures on this earth.

Have you ever been to a zoo and looked at all of the different animals that God created? There are so many unique and amazing animals. Some have horns and scales, as well as big teeth to allow them to tear flesh and plants just like dinosaurs. God created a whole world full of fantastic and interesting creatures. The next time you go to the zoo, take a closer look at all God's creatures to see how much you can learn about His creation.

7

GENESIS 8

Well, junior archaeologists, look at all the evidence you extracted last week at the dig site. You discovered how the flood began, and with the help of Dr. Moses, you dug up truth surrounding the mystery of the dinosaurs.

Now we need to find out HOW long the flood lasted. HOW did Noah know WHEN to leave the ark? And HOW did the earth change after such a devastating catastrophe?

EXAMINING THE SOIL

Are you ready to investigate HOW the earth changed as a result of the flood? Today we are going to head over to the soil pit and then to the lab with Hannah, Dr. Moses, and Dr. David Kenyon, our on-site geologist. Do you know what a geologist does? Geologists are scientists that study rocks and minerals and the way the land was formed. That is going to be very important today as we look at how creationists and naturalists think that sedimentary rocks and their many fossils formed.

Do you know what a creationist is? A creationist is a scientist who believes God's Word. A creationist studies how true science supports the Bible's record of Creation and the flood.

A naturalist believes that the earth happened over a period of time, that the sedimentary rocks and their many fossils took millions of years to form. Naturalists believe in evolution.

We need to investigate for ourselves how the mountains, canyons, valleys, and rivers were formed. Did the earth change because of a great flood?

Have you ever seen a flood on TV or in a movie? Did you notice how powerful the waters were as they rushed through a town or village carrying mud and debris? A small local flood can cause a lot of damage and destruction.

Now imagine a flood happening over the whole earth as God bursts open the deep and the floodgates of the sky. Can you imagine the force that roared behind those waters? There would be millions of tons of dirt, plants, and animals being pushed around on the earth.

Then as the waters dried up, the sediment would settle into layers. WHAT is sediment and WHAT are these layers? Check out Max and Molly's notes on the research card below.

Sedimentary Rocks, Strata, and Fossils

- Sedimentary rocks are rocks that are made of materials like bits of sand, mud, dead plants, and animals that have been transported by moving water, glaciers, or wind from one place to another.
- Strata are the layers of the earth that are made of sedimentary rock.
- Fossils are evidences of plants or animals that were buried quickly in the sediment. They are preserved in the rocks.

Let's do an experiment that shows how sediment is formed.

You will need:

a quart glass jar with a lid (like a jelly or mayonnaise jar)

½ cup dirt

¼ cup sand

¼ cup small stones or pebbles

1½ cups water

Pour your dirt into the bottom of the jar. Add sand, stones, and water. Make sure you don't fill it all the way to the top. Put the lid on tightly and shake the jar. After you have shaken the jar, set it down and watch the sediment settle. Don't shake it again.

WHAT settles first? ______________

WHAT settles last? ________________

Do the particles settle in layers? ____________________

Have you ever seen pictures of the Grand Canyon? Did you know it is almost 200 miles long and in some places it is a mile deep?

Evolutionists think it took millions of years to form all those layers of strata at the Grand Canyon. Creationists think that as the floodwaters were leaving, they cut through the layers of strata and formed canyons, gorges, and riverbeds.

Let's check out a geological catastrophe that happened in 1980.

A GEOLOGICAL CATASTROPHE

In 1980 an earthquake at Mount Saint Helens caused a huge avalanche that sent pulverized rock material down the mountain and into Spirit Lake. The avalanche material pushed up the water of Spirit Lake out of its basin, causing a tidal wave. This tidal wave stripped soil, trees, and debris off the mountain slopes and back into the lake. It also uncorked the volcano, causing it to erupt. In six minutes the explosion cloud leveled 156 square miles of forest. Needles, twigs, and smaller branches were vaporized. Mudflows formed by melted snow and ice along with volcanic ash poured into the valley, wreaking havoc for scores of miles downstream.

Geologists watched many changes that they thought would take years to happen, happen in only a matter of hours, minutes, and seconds during this catastrophe.

Mount Saint Helens shows how a geologic catastrophe can have a significant effect on earth, causing geological features such as layering of deposits, canyons, and buried forests to be formed quickly, rather than taking thousands of years as scientists used to think.

Now let's look at fossils. Did you know that there are approximately one-quarter of a million species of fossil organisms? A fossil has to be buried very quickly so that it will be preserved. Naturalists think that the layers of earth were laid slowly over long periods of time. If a plant or animal were covered slowly, then it would have rotted while it was being covered, and we would not have the whole fossils that we have today. Finding a large amount of fossils suggests that the earth's sediments were deposited very quickly, just like they would have been in the flood.

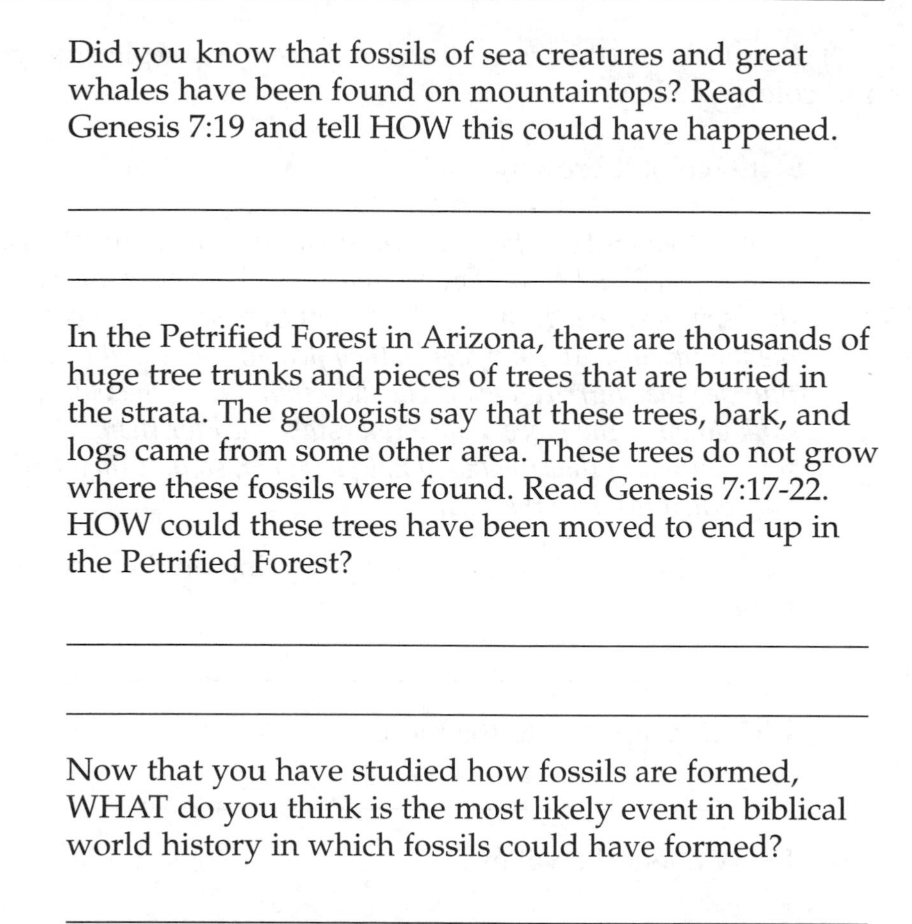

Did you know that fossils of sea creatures and great whales have been found on mountaintops? Read Genesis 7:19 and tell HOW this could have happened.

In the Petrified Forest in Arizona, there are thousands of huge tree trunks and pieces of trees that are buried in the strata. The geologists say that these trees, bark, and logs came from some other area. These trees do not grow where these fossils were found. Read Genesis 7:17-22. HOW could these trees have been moved to end up in the Petrified Forest?

Now that you have studied how fossils are formed, WHAT do you think is the most likely event in biblical world history in which fossils could have formed?

Let's look at a question that a lot of scientists ask. If there was a worldwide flood, then WHERE did all the water go?

Last week we looked at one of the scientific models, called plate tectonics. This model suggests that the earth's crust moved, which caused the hot mantle to push the ocean up on the dry land. Then, once the crust cooled back down, the floodwaters ran back into the oceans and off the earth.

What about Scripture? Let's look at Psalm 104:5-9 printed on the next page. This Scripture does not specifically say it is talking about the water from the flood, but it does offer a possible explanation.

Let's mark every reference to the following words. (Don't forget to mark pronouns!)

He, You, Your (this refers to God—draw a purple triangle and color it yellow)

earth (color it brown) water

Psalm 104:5-9 *He established the earth upon its foundations, so that it will not totter forever and ever. You covered it with the deep as with a garment; the waters were standing above the mountains. At Your rebuke they fled, at the sound of Your thunder they hurried away. The mountains rose; the valleys sank down to the place which You established for them. You set a boundary that they may not pass over, so that they will not return to cover the earth.*

WHAT happened to the waters standing on the mountains?

____

WHAT happened to the mountains?

____

HOW about the valleys?

____

WHAT do you think happened to all the water when the flood was over?

____

____

Now that you have looked at how sedimentary rocks, strata, and fossils are formed, WHAT do you believe? Do you believe that there was a worldwide flood that changed the earth? Or do you believe that the sedimentary rocks, strata, and fossils evolved slowly over a long period of time?

____

You did a wonderful job examining the soil!

To discover this week's memory verse, look at the maze below. Find the correct path through the ark, and write the words that you discover on that path on an index card. Then check your Observation Worksheets to discover the reference of your verse.

START BUT GOD SAID TO
ALL AND BEASTS REMEMBERED NOAH
THE CATTLE THE ALL AND
WERE THAT LIVED HIS SONS
WITH HIM ARK AND GOD
THE IN THE A CAUSED
SHIP PASS TO WIND THE
THE OVER THE WATER ARK
EARTH AND WIND SUBSIDED FINISH

Genesis 8: _____

SEARCHING FOR CLUES

How did you like working with Dr. Kenyon and Dr. Moses yesterday?

Wasn't that amazing learning that the Grand Canyon could have been caused by the flood in Genesis? Last week as we left Genesis 7, Noah and his family were still in the ark with the waters from the flood still covering the earth.

Let's get started today by turning to page 207 and reading Genesis 8. Mark the following key words along with their pronouns. Make sure that you mark everything that tells you WHEN with a green clock like this: Mark anything that tells you WHERE by double-underlining it in green.

Lord (God) (draw a purple triangle and color it yellow)

Noah (color it blue) earth (color it brown)

water raven (draw a black bird)

dove (draw a blue outline of a bird and leave it white)

every (color it orange) flesh (underline in pink)

Now that you have done your research, why don't you practice your memory verse? Then go with Max and Molly to the stream to look for rocks. Have you ever noticed a difference in the rocks that are in the stream and the ones that you find on the ground, other than the fact that the ones in the stream are wet? If you have a stream close by, ask a grown-up to take you. Check out the rocks that are in the stream and the rocks that are found on the ground and see if you can figure out how they are different and why.

ANOTHER FIND

"Hey, guys," Dr. Kenyon called to Molly and Max on their way back from the stream. "Come over here and tell me what you discovered about the rocks." Dr. Kenyon laughed as he watched a very wet Molly and a grinning Max head toward him. "What happened, Molly?"

Max's grin got bigger as Molly reached over and swatted at him.

"Max thinks he is soooo funny. Just as I was reaching down to pick up the coolest rock, Max yelled, 'Snake,' and I fell backwards into the water."

"Max, you didn't?" Dr. Kenyon tried to keep a straight face.

"I couldn't help it. The idea just hit me while she was picking up that rock. I didn't know she'd actually fall into the water, but you should have seen her face!"

"You just wait. When you least expect it, *revenge!*" Molly dramatically stated and then laughed. "Just keep your eyes open at all times."

"Did you bring any rocks back?" asked Dr. Kenyon.

"We sure did," replied Max. "This box has the rocks from the ground, and this box has the rocks from the stream in it."

"Okay, take out a rock from the ground and feel it. Now feel one of the rocks from the stream. How does the rock from the ground feel?"

"Kind of rough and sharp," answered Molly.

"How about the rock from the stream?"

"Smooth and kind of rounded," Max replied.

"Great! Now can you tell me why the rocks from the stream feel smooth? Think about what you learned about the water cutting through the Grand Canyon."

"I think I know." Molly's eyes lit up. "It's because the water wears down the rocks as it constantly flows over them, smoothing them out."

"Very good, Molly. Do you know what the process is called?" Dr. Kenyon paused for a minute. "It's called 'weathering.' Wind, rain, cold, running water, and plant roots can all break down and weather rocks."

"That is so cool," Max replied.

"Now are you ready to head back to Genesis and see what you can uncover today?" asked Dr. Kenyon.

Let's turn to Genesis 8 on page 207 and find out WHAT is happening on the ark. Read Genesis 8 and solve the crossword puzzle on the next page.

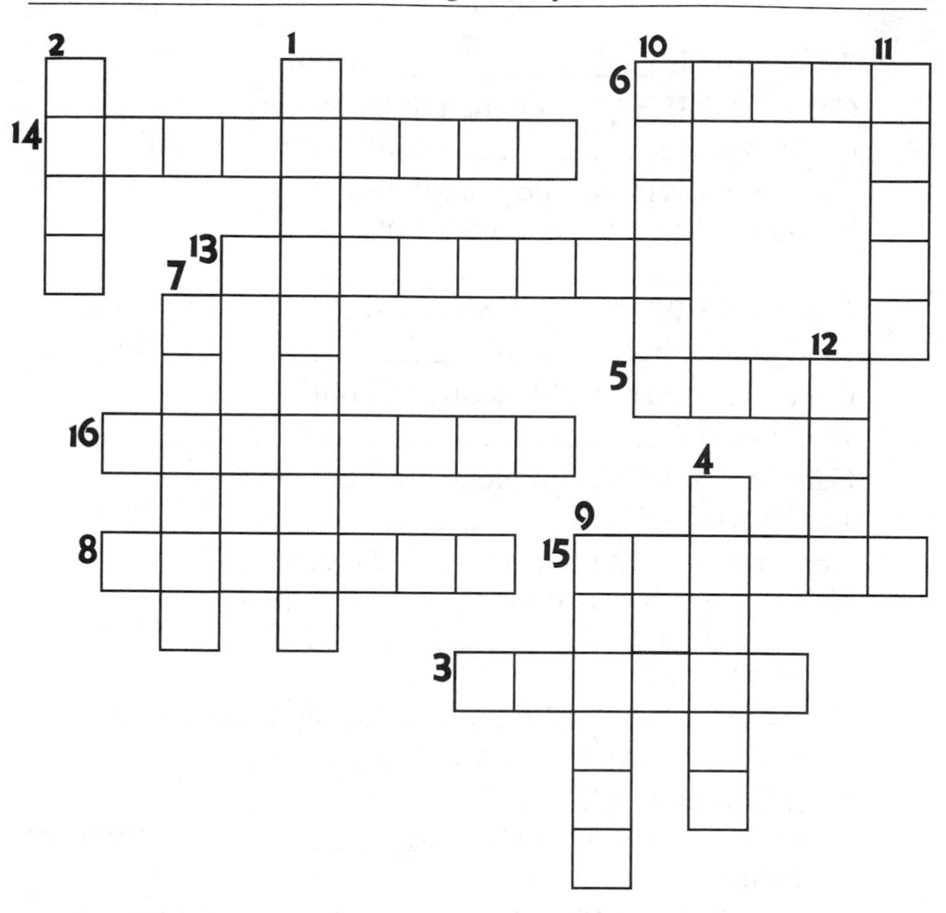

Genesis 8:1 WHAT did God do?

1. (Down) He ______________________.

WHO did God remember?

2. (Down) ______________________

3. (Across) and all the ______________________, and all the

4. (Down) ______________ that were with him in the ark.

WHAT did God do WHEN He remembered?

5. (Across) God caused a ______________ to pass over the earth.

WHAT happened when the wind passed over the earth?

6. (Across) The ______________ subsided.

Genesis 8:2 WHAT did God do to the fountains of the deep and the floodgates of the sky?

7. (Down) He __________________ them.

Genesis 8:3 WHAT happened to the water?
8. (Across) It _____________ steadily from the earth.

Genesis 8:4 WHERE did the ark rest?
9. (Down) Upon the mountains of
____

Genesis 8:6 WHAT did Noah do at the end of 40 days?
10. (Down) He opened the _________________ of the ark.

Genesis 8:7 WHAT did Noah send out?
11. (Down) A ______________________

Genesis 8:8 WHAT did Noah send out next?
12. (Down) A _____________________

Genesis 8:9 WHAT happened to the dove?
13. (Across) The dove found no resting place for the sole of her foot, so she _______________________ to him into the ark.

Genesis 8:11 WHAT did the dove bring in her beak?
14. (Across) A freshly picked _________________________

WHAT did this tell Noah?
15. (Across) That the water was ________________ from the earth.

Genesis 8:13 WHAT did Noah do when the water was dried up from the earth?
16. (Across) He removed the ________________ of the ark.

TESTING THE ARTIFACTS

"Max, are you about ready to go?" Molly asked as she watched him throw the ball for Sam to chase. "Did you forget that we get to work in the lab today?"

"I'll be ready to go in just a minute. Uncle Jake is going to come by and get Sam and take him with him on his trip into town. We didn't think it would be a good idea to let Sam loose in the lab."

"You're right about that! Sam would just love sniffing all those artifacts."

Uncle Jake walked up with Dr. Moses. "Sam, ol' buddy, how about a ride into town with Dr. Moses? Okay, you guys, make sure you stay out of trouble while I take Dr. Moses back to the university."

"It was nice to meet you, Dr. Moses. Thanks for all your help!" Max and Molly shook Dr. Moses's hand. "Maybe we'll get to come visit you at the university before we go home."

"I hope so. I had a wonderful time. You are both eager to learn, and that makes teaching so much fun. Do a good job in the lab today. See you soon."

"'Bye, Uncle Jake. 'Bye, Sam. Be a good dog! Okay, Molly, let's grab our notebooks and head to the lab."

Now that we are at the lab, we need to do some research. HOW long did the flood last? HOW long have Noah and his family been on the ark?

Let's read Genesis 8 on page 207 and look at every place you put a green clock on your Observation Worksheets that tells us WHEN the events happened. Now let's write WHAT the event was and WHEN it happened on the chart.

As you look at the chart, you need to realize that the Bible doesn't say how old Noah was when he started building the ark. But we know from Genesis 6:9-14 that it was after Noah's sons Shem, Ham, and Japheth were born. So, on your chart next to Genesis 6:14, put the ages Noah was in Genesis 5:32 and Genesis 7:11.

	Event	When
Genesis 5:32		__________ years old
Genesis 6:14		Between _______ and _________ years old
Genesis 7:11		__________ years __________ month __________ day
Genesis 7:12		__________ days __________ nights
Genesis 7:24		__________ days
Genesis 8:4		__________ month __________ day
Genesis 8:5		__________ month __________ day
Genesis 8:6		At the end of _______ days
Genesis 8:10		After _______ days
Genesis 8:12		After _______ days
Genesis 8:13		__________ years __________ month __________ day
Genesis 8:14		__________ month __________ day

Read Genesis 8:13. HOW old was Noah when the water was dried up on the earth? Put the answer in the blank labeled A below.

Read Genesis 7:6 and 7:11. HOW old was Noah when the flood began? Put the answer in the blank labeled B below.

Now take the number in blank B and subtract it from the number in blank A, and you will see HOW long Noah was on the ark.

A. ________ years - B. ________ years = ________ year

Can you imagine being on a huge boat in the middle of a devastating storm, with waves crashing, and all those animals for a whole year? Did you know that many times during a cataclysmic event animals will hover together and go into a state of hibernation? Hibernation is a state of sleep. Aren't you amazed at how God takes care of even the smallest details?

Now practice saying your memory verse. Don't you just love this verse?

> *God remembered Noah and all the beasts and all the cattle that were with him.*

God never forgets us. Even when we are in the most difficult circumstances, God is there and He remembers us!

RECORDING THE RESULTS

Now at long last the flood is over. HOW did Noah know WHEN to leave the ark? WHAT will the earth look like now that the flood is over?

Imagine coming out of the ark after a year and finding that everything had changed. Remember what we have learned about floods, earthquakes, and volcanoes. The land wouldn't look the same. Sin has once again taken its toll on the earth. Do you remember the change that happened to the earth when Adam and Eve sinned?

Look at what God said about the ground in Genesis 3:18-19.

WHAT did the earth grow after Adam and Eve sinned?

____

This is the second time we see a change in the perfect world that God created, and both times it is due to sin. Do you see how serious God takes sin? God never allows sin to go unpunished.

Let's go back and read Genesis 8 on page 208 to find out what happens now that Noah has removed the covering of the ark and the ground has dried up.

Genesis 8:15 HOW did Noah know it was okay to leave the ark?

____

Genesis 8:16 WHAT did God tell Noah?

____

Genesis 8:17 WHAT else did God tell Noah to do?
"Bring out with you every living thing of all _________."
"Be __________ and __________ on the earth."

Genesis 8:18 Did Noah obey God? __________________

Genesis 8:20 WHAT happened after they left the ark?

____

WHAT did Noah offer?

____

WHY do you think Noah did this?

____

Genesis 8:21 WHAT did the Lord do?

____

WHAT did the Lord say to Himself?
"I will never again _____________ the _____________
on account of man."
"I will never again _____________ every
_____________ _____________, as I have done."

Do you remember the key phrase that you marked in Genesis 6 and 7?

Thus Noah did; according to all that God had commanded him, so he did.

Noah did everything that God commanded. Can God say that about you?

____

Did you notice that Noah doesn't come out of the ark until God tells him to? Noah waits on God's timing and direction.

Do you ask God for direction in your life?
___ Yes ___ No

Do you wait for an answer and listen to what He says?
___ Yes ___ No

HOW does Noah begin his new life? By building an altar to worship God. Do you worship God? Do you give Him first place in your life and treat Him as holy?

Do you thank Him for bringing you safely through the storm? God provided an ark of salvation for Noah and his family to escape His judgment. God provides an ark for you, too. Let's find out how.

Noah and his family had to trust God and enter the ark in order to escape God's judgment and be saved. There was only one door, one way inside the ark, just like there is only one way for us to be saved.

> John 14:6 *Jesus said to him, "I am the way, and the truth, and the life; no one comes to the Father but through Me."*

The only way you and I can escape God's judgment is through His Son, Jesus Christ. We must come to Him, believe in Him, and receive Him as our Lord and Savior. Then we are in Christ and saved from God's judgment, just like Noah.

8

GENESIS 9

How did you like working in the lab last week? Not only did we uncover some interesting things as we tested our artifacts, but we also saw Noah, his family, and every living creature leave the ark and begin their new life.

This week we will head back to the pit to see what we can dig up about Noah's new life.

BACK IN THE PIT

As Max, Molly, and Sam headed to the dig pit, Max asked Molly, "How much dirt is in a hole ten feet long by five feet wide and two feet deep?"

"Ummm, let me see...10 x 5 x 2 is 100 cubic feet," exclaimed Molly.

Max burst out laughing. "Gotcha! The answer is *none*. There isn't any dirt in a hole. It's *empty!*"

"Now that's two I owe you, Max," squealed Molly.

Uncle Jake walked up. "Are you guys ready to head back to the pit?"

How about you? Let's talk to our "site boss," and then we can get started. Turn to page 209 and read Genesis 9. Let's mark our maps by looking for the following key words.

Lord (God) (draw a purple triangle and color it yellow)

Noah (color it blue) earth (color it brown)

all (color it green and box it in yellow)

every (color it orange)

covenant (color it red and box it in yellow)

blood (draw in red)

sign

As we continue to dig up truth this week, we will discover WHY God put the rainbow in the clouds. Take a look at the rainbow to find this week's memory verse.

Each ray of the rainbow has words from your memory verse in it. Start with the top ray and the first word, *And.* Place the word *And* on the first blank under the verse. Then choose the first word on the second ray, and place it in the next blank, and then do the same thing for the third ray. Then go back and do the same thing again, choosing the second word from each ray. Continue to do this until you have discovered your memory verse. When you have uncovered your verse, look in chapter 9 to find the reference that goes with it.

AND REMEMBER WHICH ME AND CREATURE FLESH AGAIN WATER FLOOD ALL

I MY IS AND EVERY OF AND SHALL BECOME TO FLESH

WILL COVENANT BETWEEN YOU LIVING ALL NEVER THE A DESTROY

And ___ _______ ______________ _______

______________, __________ _____

______________ ______ ________ ________

_____ __________ ______________

______________ ______ ________ ________;

________ _________ __________ ________

______ ___________ _____________ _____

_____________ _____ _____________ _____

___________.

Genesis 9: ____

Now what do you need to do? How many times?

MORE DIGGING

"Uncle Jake, Uncle Jake," Molly cried out excitedly. "Come quick. I think I found something!"

Uncle Jake and William both climbed down into the pit.

"You're right, Molly. I think you may have something there. It could be another wall, or maybe a pillar. Mary Frances, why don't you get some shots as we continue to scrape away the dirt?"

"I'll be right over," Mary Frances called out.

What do you think it might be? Help Molly and Max scrape away the dirt by turning to Genesis 9 on page 209. We need to ask the 5 W's and an H questions as we uncover our find.

Genesis 9:1 WHAT did God do to Noah and his sons?
________________ them

WHAT command does God give them?
Be ________________ and ______________ and
___________ the __________________.
Have you seen this command before?

Genesis 9:2 WHAT does God put on every beast, bird, creeping thing, and fish? The __________ of you and the ___________ of you. Into your _____________ they are ____________.

Genesis 9:3 WHAT is to be food for them?

Every ______________ thing that is ___________.
Genesis 9:4 WHAT are they not to eat?
___________ with its __________, its ___________

Let's sift through the soil. Before the flood, man could eat plants. After the flood we see God telling Noah and his sons that they can eat meat also. But they are not to eat the flesh with the blood.

Genesis 9:5 WHAT will God require from every man?
The ________________ of ____________

Genesis 9:6 If you shed a man's blood, WHAT will happen to you?
By man his ______________ shall be ________________.

WHY? Because, God made man in the _______________ of __________.

Genesis 9:7 WHAT does God want them to do?
______________________ the earth abundantly

Now record your find. Take every answer that fits on an individual blank and find it in the word search below.

L	W	G	B	W	V	J	D	R	K	W	C
I	U	P	N	Y	F	Z	V	M	A	N	T
F	D	F	O	L	Z	G	G	I	V	E	N
E	Z	M	T	P	N	O	X	Z	R	H	F
J	L	D	T	I	U	D	L	R	T	S	I
F	D	O	V	T	U	L	O	R	C	E	L
Q	Z	O	K	L	S	R	A	V	U	L	L
N	M	L	A	U	U	E	F	T	C	F	A
B	F	B	L	M	D	E	S	S	E	L	B
B	Y	X	G	N	E	G	A	M	I	O	T
F	N	M	A	F	G	Q	K	V	R	N	S
D	E	H	S	O	D	Q	E	W	I	L	D

Fantastic!

SCRAPING AWAY THE DIRT

It looks like you're getting a little sunburned. Let's put on some more sunscreen before we climb back into the pit. As we continue to scrape away the dirt, we need to take a closer look at WHAT God means in Genesis 9:6 when He talks about man shedding man's blood. WHAT is it called when a man kills another man?

____

WHAT is murder? Do you know? To murder is to kill someone on purpose. Sometimes a person is killed, but it is an accident. God handles an accidental killing different than He does a murder.

Let's do some cross-referencing to see what God's Word has to say about killing a man made in His image.

Look up and read Exodus 20:13. WHAT does God say?

____

Read Exodus 21:12-14.
Exodus 21:12 Does this sound like murder or an accidental killing?

____

WHAT is the punishment for the one who murders a man?

____

Exodus 21:13 WHAT does this sound like—murder or an accidental killing? ____________________

WHAT is the punishment for the one who doesn't intentionally kill a man? ______________________________

Exodus 21:14 The Hebrew word for *presumptuously* is *zud,* or *zid,* and it means "to boil up, to seethe, to act proudly or rebelliously."

So WHAT kind of killing is this—a murder or an accident? ______________________________

WHAT is the consequence? ______________________________

Look up and read Leviticus 24:17-21.
Leviticus 24:17 WHAT is to happen to a man who takes the life of a human being?

____

Leviticus 24:18 WHAT is to happen to the one who takes the life of an animal?

____

Leviticus 24:19-20 WHAT is to happen to a man who injures his neighbor?

____

Does God give the same punishment for killing an animal that He does for killing a human being?

____

Do you see how important human beings are to God?

____

Does God value people more than animals?

____

WHY?

____

____

Numbers 35:9-34 is a passage where God tells Moses what to tell the sons of Israel concerning cities of refuge for those who have accidentally killed someone, and what to do with those who have committed murder. Today we are only going to look at part of this passage. Read Numbers 35:30-34.

Numbers 35:30 WHEN is a murderer to be put to death?
At the evidence of ____________________
No person shall be put to death on the
____________________ of ______________
____

Verses 31 and 32 show us how to deal with a murderer and someone who accidentally kills someone. WHY are you to put a murderer to death and exile someone who kills accidentally? Look at verses 33 and 34. Because
b _ _ _ _ p _ _ _ _ _ _ _ _ the land.

The only way the land can be expiated (have atonement made, or forgiveness) for the blood shed on it is to do WHAT? Look at verse 33.

____

By digging in God's Word we have seen that God places a very high value on human beings. He created us in His image. Murder pollutes the land unless we put the murderer to death.

Do you know what capital punishment is? That's when a person who has been found guilty in a court of law is put to death for killing another person. Is that biblical? ___ Yes ___ No

There are a lot of people who don't think we should practice capital punishment today. From what you have studied in God's Word, WHAT do you think and WHY?

____

____

WHAT is abortion? Do you know? It's when a pregnant woman decides to have her baby killed before it is born.

Some people claim that a baby isn't really a baby until it is born. WHAT does God say? Look up and read Psalm 139:13-14.

Did God create that baby inside the mother?
___ Yes ___ No

Do you think God considers that baby to be a baby before it is born? ___ Yes ___ No

So WHAT do you think? Is abortion murder?
___ Yes ___ No

WHAT do you think about our land? Is it polluted?
___ Yes ___ No

We have already seen God judge the land by sending a flood. Since we live in a polluted world, will God judge the earth again? Yes, He will. Will God send another flood? We'll find out tomorrow as we continue to scrape away the dirt.

ANOTHER BIG FIND!

"Oh, man, look at that!" Max exclaimed. "Isn't that cool?"

"It sure is," replied Uncle Jake. "You and Molly have just uncovered a big find! That looks like a pillar. We may be onto something here."

Good work, junior archaeologists. Let's continue to expose this awesome discovery by turning to page 210 and reading Genesis 9:8-17.

> Genesis 9:9-10 WHAT is God going to establish with Noah and his descendants, and with every living creature of the earth?
>
> ____

WHAT is a covenant? Do you know? The Hebrew word for *covenant* is *berith,* and it is pronounced *ber-eeth'*. A covenant is a compact made by passing between pieces of flesh. It is a treaty, an alliance, a pledge, or agreement. A covenant is a lifelong promise that can never be broken.

Do you remember marking this word in Genesis 6? Genesis 6 is the first time that God uses this word *covenant.* Turn back to Genesis 6:18-19. God is establishing His covenant with Noah and his family, promising to keep them alive during the flood. Now in chapter 9 we see God is going to make a promise to Noah, his descendants, and all the living creatures on earth. Let's find out more about God's promise.

Genesis 9:11 WHAT is the promise (covenant) that God made?

____

Genesis 9:12-13 WHAT sign did God give to remind Noah, his future generations, and every living creature of this promise?

____

Genesis 9:14 WHEN will the bow be seen?

____

Genesis 9:15 WHAT will the bow remind God of?

____

Genesis 9:16 HOW long will this covenant last?

____

Looking back at the definition of *covenant,* can a covenant ever be broken? ___ Yes ___ No

Did God keep His covenant with Noah in Genesis 6? Did He bring Noah, his family, and all the living creatures on the ark through the flood safely? ____________

Can God lie? NO! God cannot lie. What He says He will do. God always keeps His promises. He is faithful!

After the devastating flood, God in His love and mercy gives Noah a promise to never again destroy the world by water. He seals His promise by putting a bow in the clouds. Have you ever seen a rainbow? ______________

WHEN did it appear? ____________________________

If you had never seen rain before the flood, HOW do you think you would feel the next time it rained? Would you be a little scared and anxious? WHY?

____

Rainbows appear when it rains. They are to remind God of His covenant. Do you think they also reminded Noah and his family that God would keep them safe so they wouldn't be frightened the next time it rained?

Isn't that amazing that a holy and awesome God would love us enough to make us a promise—one that could never be broken?

Yesterday we talked about HOW God would judge the earth next time. After all you have learned today, will God send another flood to judge the earth? __________

HOW will God judge the earth the next time?

____

If you don't know the answer to this question, look up and read 2 Peter 3:10 to find the answer.

You have discovered a *big find!* God is a promise-keeping God. How about you? Do you keep your promises?

Now head to the showers. In honor of your big discovery, we are going to have a wienie roast tonight!

EXPOSING ANOTHER LAYER

"You almost have that pillar uncovered," William told Max and Molly as they carefully scraped the dirt off the pillar with their trowels and brushes.

"Please pass the canteen, Max. I am so thirsty," sighed Molly.

"Me, too," replied Max. "Ahh, that tastes so good!"

Are you ready to do a little more scraping? Let's turn to page 211 to uncover the rest of Genesis 9. Let's read Genesis 9:18-24.

Genesis 9:18 WHO are Noah's sons?

____

WHO was Ham's son?

____

Genesis 9:19 HOW was the whole earth populated?

____

Genesis 9:20 WHAT does Noah do?

____

Genesis 9:21 WHAT happens to Noah?

____

Genesis 9:22 WHO finds Noah?

____

WHAT does he do?

____

Genesis 9:23 WHAT do Shem and Japheth do?

____

Genesis 9:24-27 WHAT is Noah's response? WHOM does he bless?

____

WHOM does he curse?

____

Genesis 9:28 HOW long does Noah live after the flood?

____

Genesis 9:29 HOW old is Noah when he dies?

____

As we examine our findings, we see that Noah and his sons have obeyed God and populated the earth. God has called Noah a righteous man, but is Noah perfect? No, he isn't. He makes mistakes just like we do. WHAT do we do when we make a mistake? (Remember 1 John 1:9.) ____

Ham ran to tell his brothers about Noah's mistake. Was that the right thing to do? ___ Yes ___ No

Shem and Japheth did not want to dishonor their father, so they walked into his room backward in order to cover him.

Do you honor your parents? ___ Yes ___ No

WHAT happened to Ham? ______________________________

WHAT about Shem and Japheth? ______________________

Now head for the shade to drink that nice, cold lemonade. Think about how you treat your parents. Do you make fun of your parents? Do you speak with respect, or with an exasperated tone? Do you do what they tell you to, or do you argue to get your way? Remember Shem and Japheth's blessing and Ham's curse. Why don't you say your verse to a friend or grown-up? Then lie back and drink that lemonade.

9

GENESIS 10–11

Can you believe it? This is our last week at the dig site. As we finish up our digging, we need to help tag the artifacts that we have uncovered. We also need to find out WHERE all the different nations came from. If everyone came from Adam through Noah, then WHY are there so many different languages? Let's find out.

LOOSENING THE DIRT

"Hey, Molly, did you hear that clink?" Max asked as he tapped his trowel on the floor of the dirt pit.

"I sure did. Let's use our *patish* to loosen the dirt. I think you might have found something, Max."

"Uncle Jake was right. I think we are onto something big: first the stone wall, then the pillar, and I wonder what this could be?"

"I don't know, but let's keep working and find out."

Let's get busy. Turn to page 213 on your Observation Worksheets and read Genesis 10. Now mark the following key words and key phrases. Mark anything that tells you WHEN with a clock like this: Mark anything that tells you WHERE by double-underlining it in green.

Shem (draw a blue) Ham (draw a green)

Japheth (draw an orange) the earth (color it brown)

nations (color it green and underline it in brown)

after the flood (color it orange and put a green clock over it)

according to their language (color it pink)

by their lands (circle it in blue)

Now let's find your memory verse. Look at the broken pieces of pottery on the next page and see if you can figure out how they would fit together to make a whole piece of pottery. We have labeled each piece (shard) with a phrase or a word. So as you figure out how they should fit together, look at the picture of the whole plate. Try to figure out how the broken pieces would fit on the whole plate. Write the word or phrase on the matching piece on the whole plate. Then write them in order on the blanks below. If a phrase is on a shard, then it will fit on one blank. We've done the first one for you.

They said, ____________________ __________________

__________________________ __________________________

________________________________ __________________________

_________________________ ________________________________

___________________________ ____________________

__________________ __________________________

______________________ ___________________________________

___________________________ ______________________________.

Genesis 11: _____

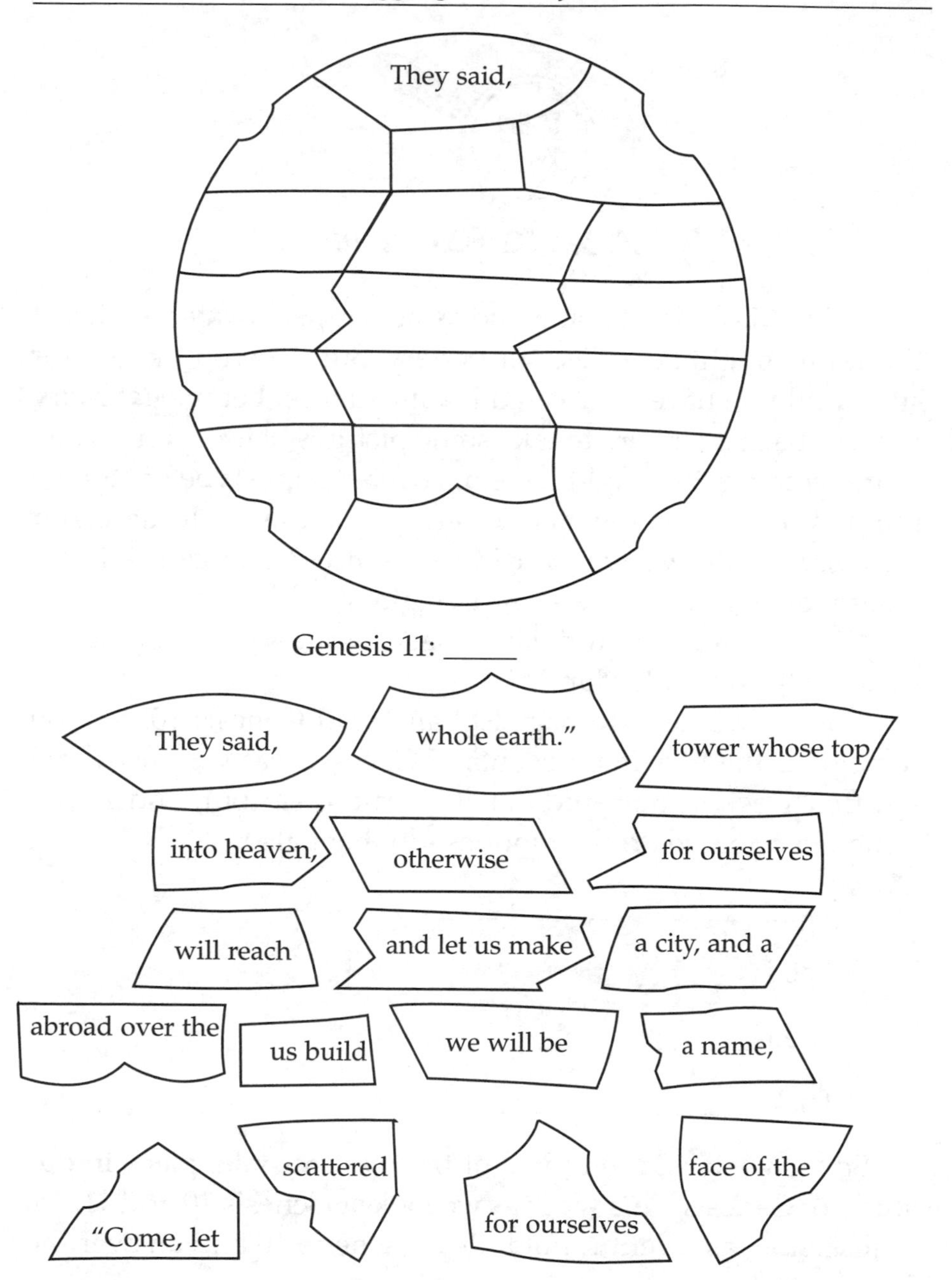
They said,
Genesis 11: _____
They said,
whole earth."
tower whose top
into heaven,
otherwise
for ourselves
will reach
and let us make
a city, and a
abroad over the
us build
we will be
a name,
"Come, let
scattered
for ourselves
face of the

LOOKING FOR CLUES

"Well, Max," Uncle Jake said as he scraped away the dirt, "I think this might be a piece of pottery. But we won't know for sure until you have uncovered it a little more. Let me get Mary Frances back over here to take some pictures before you do any more scraping. We might have uncovered some type of storage room. Why don't you and Molly go talk with Jordan, our ceramist, while we wait on Mary Frances? She can tell you what we might find as we keep digging."

"That sounds like fun, Uncle Jake," said Molly. "Come on, Max. Let's go find Jordan."

Now as we head to page 213 and read Genesis 10, do you remember the four main events of Genesis that we uncovered the first week of our study? Let's write them out, and if you remember how to do the motions, do them also:

C ___ ___ ___ ___ ___ ___ ___

The f ___ ___ ___

The f ___ ___ ___ ___

The n ___ ___ ___ ___ ___ ___

So far we have seen three of these events take place in our study of Genesis. This week as we look at Genesis 10 and 11, we will see the last event unfold. Read Genesis 10 and answer the 5 W's and an H.

Genesis 10:1 WHAT is Genesis 10 the records of?

____

WHEN did Shem, Ham, and Japheth have their sons?

____

Genesis 10:5 This is the first time we see the word *nations.* HOW were the nations separated?

____

Let's make a list of what we learn from marking *the earth.*

FIELD NOTEBOOK

The Earth:

Genesis 10:8 ____________ became a mighty ____________ on the earth.

Genesis 10:25 In ________________ days the earth was ___________________.

Genesis 10:32 The ________________ were separated on the earth ______________ the ____________.

Genesis 10 gives us the generations of Shem, Ham, and Japheth's sons, and for the first time we see that there are nations. The people are separated by their lands, and according to their language and their families. WHEN did this happen? Have we seen anyone speaking a different language? Have we seen any nations? So WHAT happened between Genesis 9 and Genesis 10 to bring about these changes?

Do you remember that Genesis 1 was an overview, the big picture of Creation, and then Genesis 2 filled in the details of Creation? The same thing happens in Genesis 10 and 11. Genesis 10 gives us the big picture, the overview, and Genesis 11 will fill in the details. Tomorrow as we look at Genesis 11, we will find out HOW these nations came about.

EXTRACTING A FIND

"Hey, guys," asked Uncle Jake, "did Jordan give you some pointers on pottery?"

"She sure did," answered Molly. "She told us that one of her jobs was to piece together the broken shards so that she can reconstruct what the original object looked like. She said it's kind of like working a jigsaw puzzle."

Max looked at Uncle Jake. "She's going to let us watch her work on some different pieces after we finish in the pit today."

"That's great! Are you ready to go uncover some more of your find? Mary Frances is finished, so you can get back to work."

Let's turn to Genesis 11 on page 216 and read our Observation Worksheets. Now mark the key words and key phrases below. Mark anything that tells you WHEN with a clock like this: Mark anything that tells you WHERE by double-underlining it in green.

Shem (draw a blue) city

after the flood (color it orange and put a green clock over it) language (color it pink) the whole earth (color it brown)

Peleg (draw a red)

the records of the generations of (color it yellow)

Now say your memory verse three times in a row, three times today!

RECONSTRUCTING THE PIECES

"Wow, Uncle Jake, just look at that!" cried an astonished Max.

"It looks like you and Molly have uncovered some type of storeroom, Max. Look at all of this pottery, and some of it is still in one piece. Jordan is going to flip when she sees this."

"Can we go tell her?" Molly asked.

"Sure, and while you're telling Jordan, tell Mary Frances we'll need more pictures. It's very important that we document every step of our excavation."

Now let's see what we will discover today. Turn to page 216 to Genesis 11 on your Observation Worksheets and read Genesis 11:1-9.

Genesis 11:1 WHAT do we see about the whole earth?

____

Genesis 11:2 WHERE did they settle?

____

Genesis 11:3 WHAT did they make? ________________

HOW did they make them?

____

Genesis 11:4 WHAT did they use the bricks for?

____

WHY? ____

Genesis 11:5 WHAT did the Lord come down to see?

____

Genesis 11:6 WHAT did the Lord notice about them?
They are ________ ______________, and they all have the ____________ ____________________.
Now nothing which they purpose to do will be ____________________ for them.

Genesis 11:7 WHAT did God do?

____

Genesis 11:8 WHAT did God do next?

____

WHAT did the people do?

____

Genesis 11:9 WHERE did God confuse their language?

____

Now we have all the pieces. The people decided to build a city that would reach heaven in order to make a name for themselves.

Are we to make a name for ourselves, or are we to glorify God's name? ______________________________

These people were rebelling against God by wanting to be great apart from God. They were focused on themselves, not on God. So God came down and confused their language. It's kind of hard to build a great city if you can't understand each other, isn't it?

Now go back to Genesis 9:1. WHAT did God tell them to do? "Be fruitful and multiply, and fill the earth." Had they multiplied? ___ Yes ___ No

Had they filled the earth, or were they all living together in the same place? ______________________________

They were disobeying God. They had not filled the earth like God told them to. HOW did God achieve His will (get them to fill the earth)?

____

God always achieves His purpose even when we get in the way. He is God and rules over everything. All power belongs to Him. We can choose to obey God and follow Him, or we can choose to do things our way. But in the end, God's will is what will prevail because He is God and we are only man.

Now let's go watch Jordan as she works on piecing together some of the broken shards.

RECORDING OUR ARTIFACTS

Well, junior archaeologists, it's our last day on the dig. We have learned so much. It has been quite an adventure. Let's go help Molly and Max learn how to tag all the artifacts that we have discovered on this dig. But before we get started, why don't you thank God for the awesome privilege of taking this adventure in His Word?

Now, let's start tagging those artifacts. Take a look at the map below to see WHERE Shem, Ham, and Japheth's descendants were scattered. Color Shem's area blue, along with his descendants who are listed in Genesis 10:22-29. Color Ham's area green, along with his descendants listed in Genesis 10:6-7, and color Japheth's area and his descendants listed in Genesis 10:2-4 orange. Then turn to Genesis 11 on page 217 and read Genesis 11:10-32.

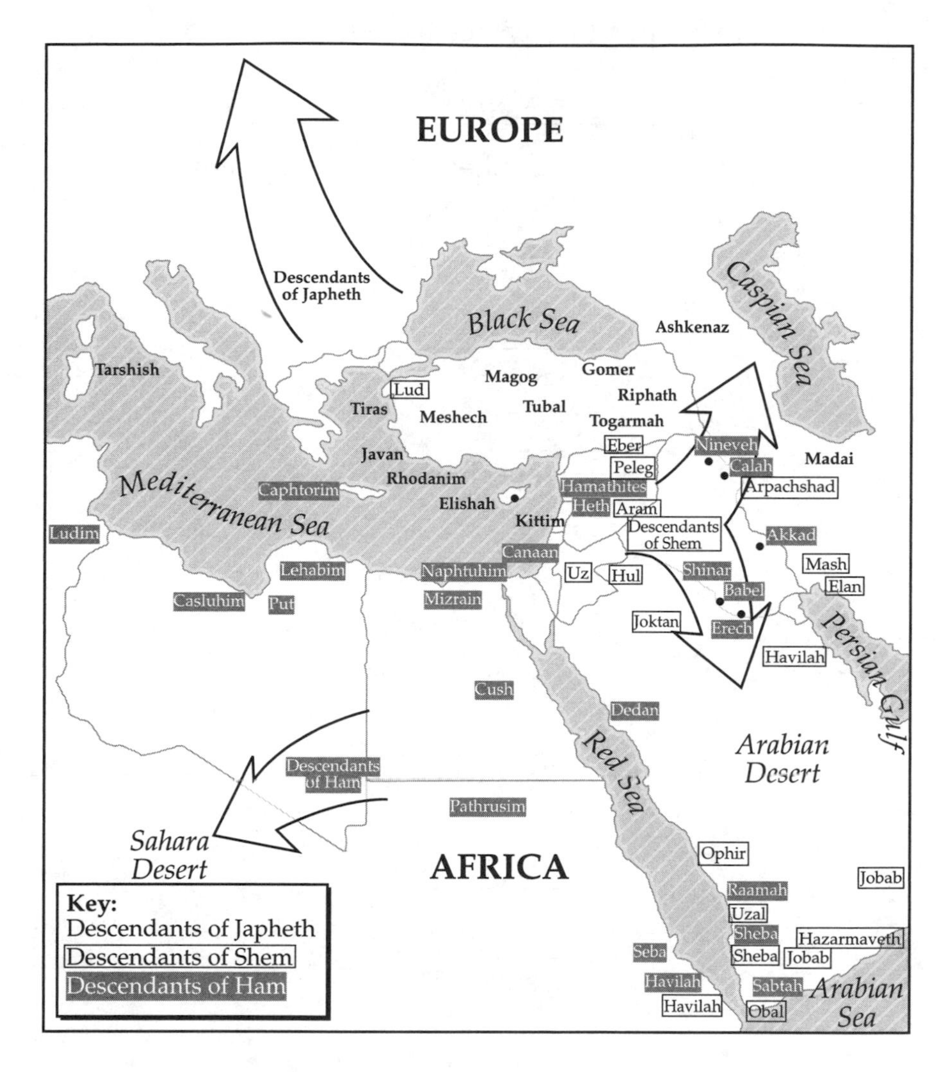

Genesis 11:10 WHOSE records of generations are these?

____

WHEN did Shem have Arpachshad?

____

Now fill in Shem's family tree below.

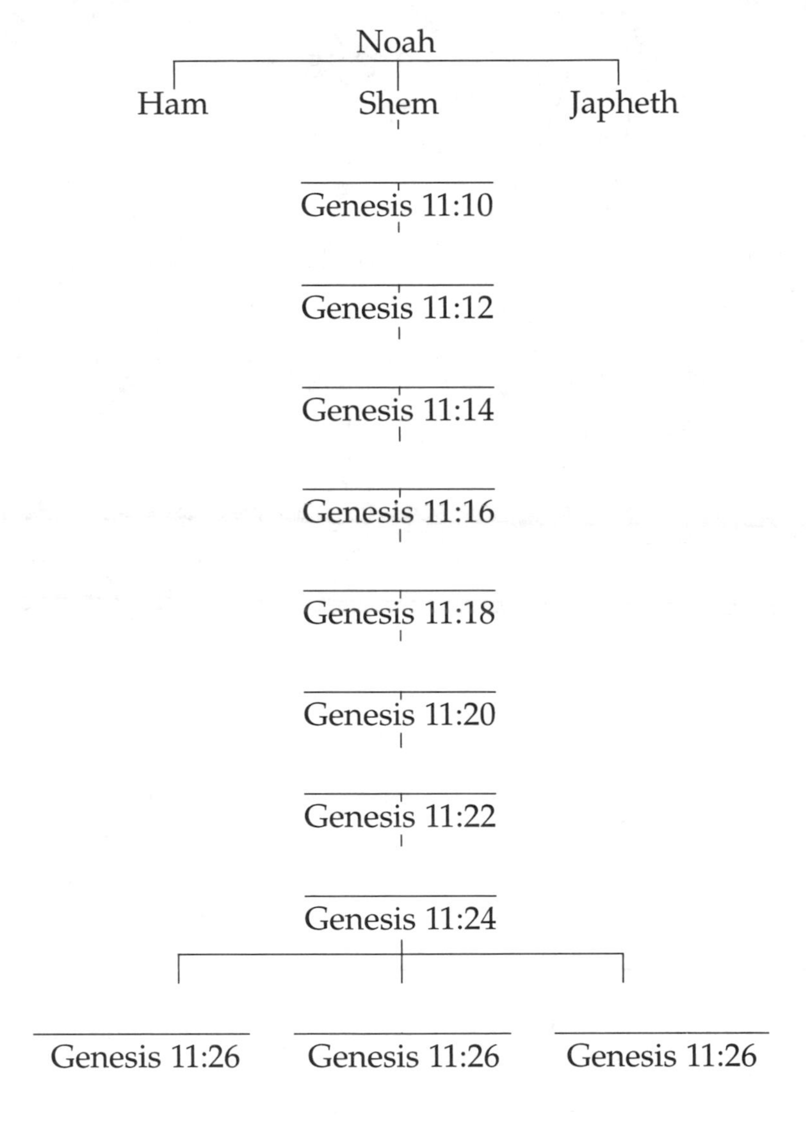

Go back and look at how long all of Shem's descendants lived after having their children. Is man living a longer life or a shorter life after the flood? If you can't remember how long man lived before the flood, check out some of the ages in Genesis 5.

____

Genesis 11:27 WHO were Terah's sons?

____

Genesis 11:28 WHERE did Terah live?

____

Genesis 11:29 WHO was Abram's wife?

____

Genesis 11:31 WHERE was Terah headed?

____

Genesis 11:32 WHERE did Terah die?

____

Who are the last people listed on Shem's family tree?

____

This is not the end of Shem's descendants. They are just the last ones listed in Genesis 11. We'll discover more about Shem's descendants as we continue our adventure in God's Word.

You did it! You have just dug up God's truths in Genesis Part Two. We are soooooo proud of you! Now let's head to the campsite. Uncle Jake has a farewell party planned just for you!

BACK AT THE CAMPSITE

Can you believe our work on Genesis Part Two is done? You did an *amazing* job! Just look at all you have discovered. You know WHAT happened to God's perfect world, WHY Adam and Eve were sent out of the garden, WHY God flooded the earth, WHOM He saved, and WHY He saved them. You also uncovered WHY we speak different languages today and live in different countries. You know the four major events that make up the first half of the Book of Genesis. All that hard work really paid off!

You also saw the very first promise of our Redeemer, Jesus Christ, who would die to pay the price of our sins. WHAT an awesome and loving God to provide a way of escape for you and me!

Don't forget to fill out the card in the back of the book. We want to send you a special certificate for helping us dig up the truth of Genesis Part Two. Now let's go sing some songs and eat those s'mores. See you real soon!

PUZZLE ANSWERS

PAGE 10

The Lord God planted a garden toward the east, in Eden; and there He placed the man whom He had formed.

Genesis 2 : 8

PAGE 25

The Lord God commanded the man, saying, "From any tree of the garden you may eat freely; but from the tree of the knowledge of good and evil you shall not eat, for in the day that you eat from it you will surely die" (Genesis 2:16-17).

PAGE 47

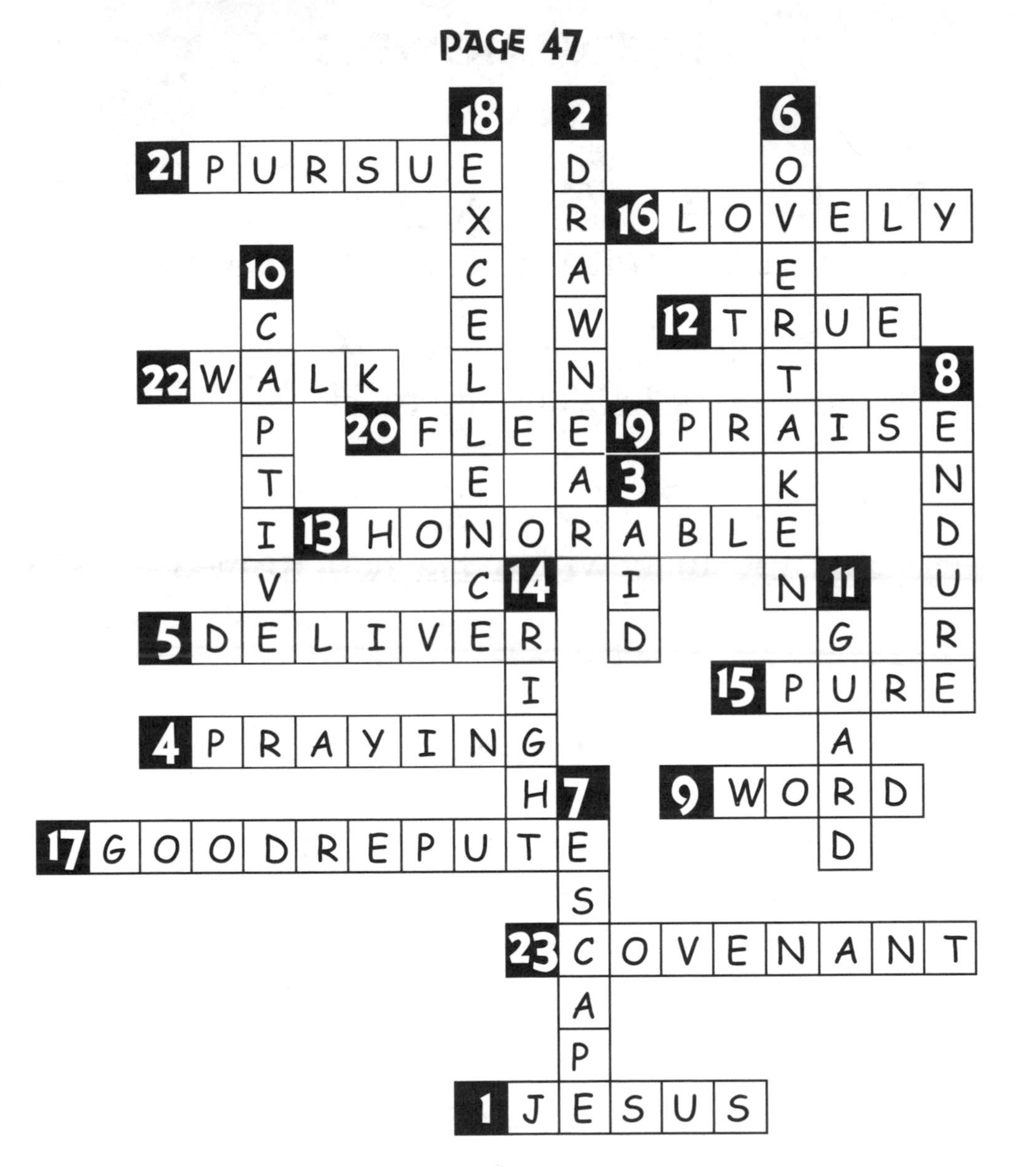

PAGE 52

THE LORD GOD MADE
GARMENTS OF SKIN FOR
ADAM AND HIS WIFE, AND
CLOTHED THEM. Genesis 3:21

PAGE 78

Abel, on his part also brought of the firstlings of his flocks and of their fat portions. And the Lord had regard for Abel and his offering; but for Cain and his offering He had no regard. So Cain became very angry and his countenance fell.

Genesis 4:4-5

PAGE 99

Then the Lord saw that the wickedness of man was great on the earth, and that every intent of the thoughts of his heart was only evil continually.

Genesis 6:5

PAGE 103

C	R	E	E	P	I	N	G	T	H	I	N	G	S
R	T	P	F	F	G	R	I	E	V	E	D	R	S
E	R	E	H	L	M	I	L	I	H	P	E	N	E
A	A	C	C	O	V	E	N	A	N	T	S	W	N
T	E	N	E	O	E	A	R	T	H	V	T	A	D
E	H	E	T	D	M	E	N	G	L	S	R	T	E
D	Y	L	P	I	T	L	U	M	P	F	O	E	K
A	B	O	U	S	L	A	M	I	N	A	Y	R	C
M	L	I	R	D	D	H	R	H	S	E	L	F	I
Y	O	V	R	M	B	I	R	D	S	E	D	N	W
Y	R	R	O	S	T	R	I	V	E	B	L	O	T
B	D	K	C	W	L	I	X	I	A	C	J	X	A

PAGE 115

Thus He blotted out every living thing that was upon the face of the land, from man to animals to creeping things and to birds of the sky, and they were blotted out from the earth; and only Noah was left, together with those that were with him in the ark.

Genesis 7:23

PAGE 141

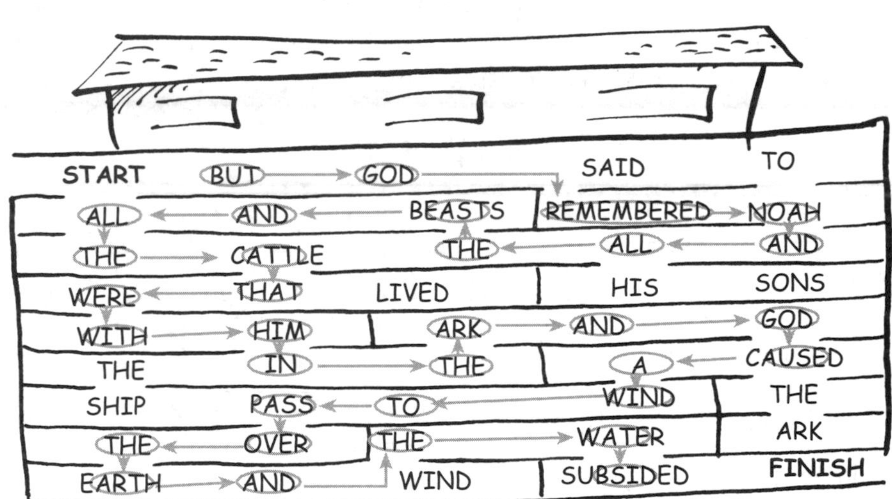

Genesis 8:1

PAGE 145

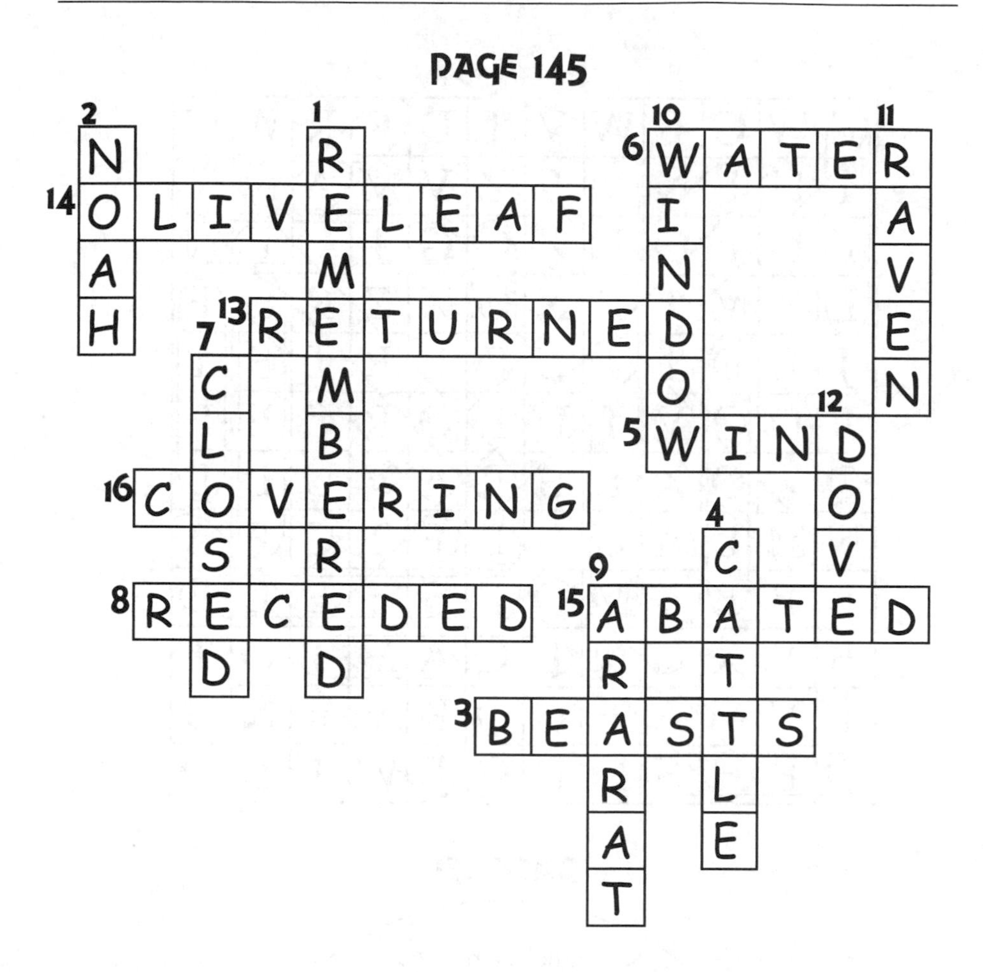

PAGE 155

And I will remember My covenant, which is between Me and you and every living creature of all flesh; and never again shall the water become a flood to destroy all flesh.

Genesis 9:15

PAGE 157

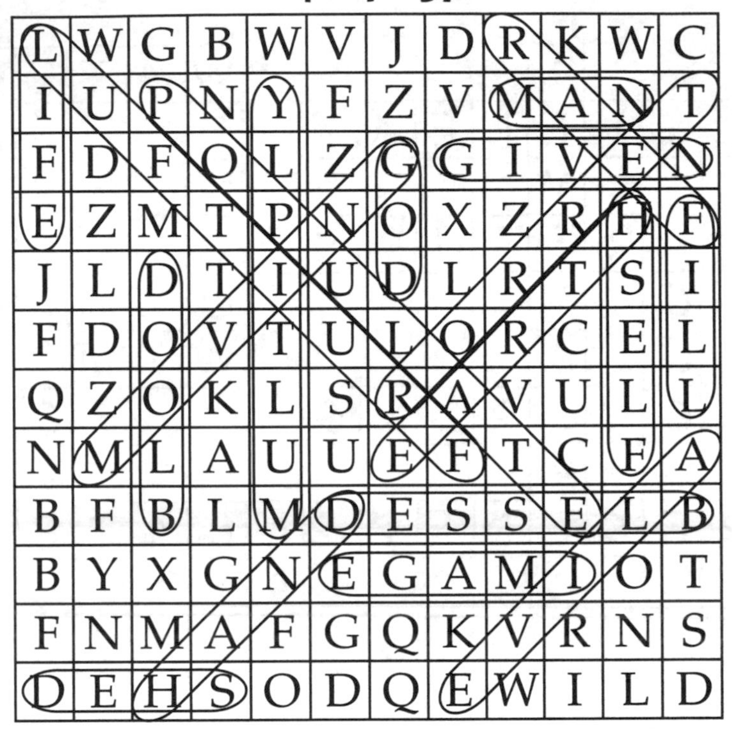

PAGE 171

Genesis 11:4

OBSERVATION WORKSHEETS
GENESIS 2-11

Chapter 2

1 Thus the heavens and the earth were completed, and all *their* hosts.

2 By *the* seventh day God completed His work which He had done, and He rested on the seventh day from all His work which He had done.

3 Then God blessed the seventh day and sanctified it, because in it He rested from all His work which God had created and made.

4 This is the account of the heavens and the earth when they were created, in the day that the LORD God made earth and heaven.

5 Now no shrub of the field was yet in the earth, and no plant of the field had yet sprouted, for the LORD God had not sent rain upon the earth, and there was no man to cultivate the ground.

6 But a mist used to rise from the earth and water the whole surface of the ground.

7 Then the LORD God formed man of dust from the ground, and breathed into his nostrils the breath of life; and man became a living being.

8 The LORD God planted a *garden* toward the east, in Eden; and there He placed the man whom He had formed.

9 Out of the ground the LORD God caused to grow *every* tree that is pleasing to the sight and good for food; *the* tree of life also in the midst of the garden, and the tree of the knowledge of good and evil.

10 Now a *river* flowed out of Eden to water the garden; and from there it divided and became four rivers.

11 The name of the first is Pishon; it flows around the whole land of *Havilah*, where there is gold.

12 The gold of that land is good; the dellium and the onyx stone are there.

13 The name of the second river is Gihon; it flows around the whole land of Cush.

14 The name of the third river is *Tigris*; it flows east of Assyria. And the fourth river is the *Euphrates*.

15 Then the LORD God took the man and put him into the garden of Eden to cultivate it and keep it.

16 The LORD God *commanded* the man, saying, "From any tree of the garden you may eat freely;

17 but from the tree of the knowledge of good and evil you shall not eat, for in the day that you eat from it *you* will surely die."

18 Then the LORD God said, "It is not good for the man to be alone; *I* will make him a helper suitable for him."

19 *Out* of the ground the LORD God formed every beast of the field and every bird of the sky, and *brought them* to the man to see what he would call them; and whatever the man called a living creature, that was its name.

20 The man gave names to all the cattle, and to the birds of the sky, and to every beast of the field, but for Adam there was not found *a* helper suitable for him.

21 So the LORD God caused a *deep* sleep to fall upon the man, and he slept; then He took one of his ribs and closed up the flesh at that place.

22 The LORD God fashioned into a woman *the* rib which He had taken from the man, and brought her to the man.

23 The man said,

"*This* is now bone of my bones,

And flesh of my flesh;

She shall be called Woman,

Because she was taken out of Man."

24 *For* this reason a man shall leave his father and his mother, and be joined to his wife; and they shall become one flesh.

25 *And* the man and his wife were both naked and were not ashamed.

Chapter 3

1 Now the serpent was more crafty than any beast of the field which the LORD God had made. And he said to the woman, "Indeed, has God said, 'You shall not eat from any tree of the garden'?"

2 The woman said to the serpent, "From the fruit of the trees of the garden we may eat;

3 but from the fruit of the tree which is in the middle of the garden, God has said, 'You shall not eat from it or touch it, or you will die.'"

4 The serpent said to the woman, "You surely will not die!

5 "For God knows that in the day you eat from it your eyes will be opened, and you will be like God, knowing good and evil."

6 When the woman saw that the tree was good for food, and that it was a delight to the eyes, and that the tree was desirable to make *one* wise, she took from its fruit and ate; and she gave also to her husband with her, and he ate.

7 Then the eyes of both of them were opened, and they knew that they were naked; and they sewed fig leaves together and made themselves loin coverings.

8 They heard the sound of the LORD God walking in the garden in the cool of the day, and the man and his wife hid themselves from the presence of the LORD God among the trees of the garden.

9 Then the LORD God called to the man, and said to him, "Where are you?"

10 He said, "I heard the sound of You in the garden, and I was afraid because I was naked; so I hid myself."

11 And He said, "Who told you that you were naked? Have you eaten from the tree of which I commanded you not to eat?"

12 The man said, "The woman whom You gave *to be* with me, she gave me from the tree, and I ate."

13 Then the LORD God said to the woman, "What is this you have done?" And the woman said, "The serpent deceived me, and I ate."

14 The LORD God said to the serpent,

"Because you have done this,
Cursed are you more than all cattle,
And more than every beast of the field;
On your belly you will go,
And dust you will eat
All the days of your life;

15 And I will put enmity
Between you and the woman,
And between your seed and her seed;
He shall bruise you on the head,
And you shall bruise him on the heel."

16 To the woman He said,

"I will greatly multiply

Your pain in childbirth,

In pain you will bring forth children;

Yet your desire will be for your husband,

And he will rule over you."

17 Then to Adam He said, "Because you have listened to the voice of your wife, and have eaten from the tree about which I commanded you, saying, 'You shall not eat from it';

Cursed is the ground because of you;

In toil you will eat of it

All the days of your life.

18 "Both thorns and thistles it shall grow for you;

And you will eat the plants of the field;

19 By the sweat of your face

You will eat bread,

Till you return to the ground,

Because from it you were taken;

For you are dust,

And to dust you shall return."

20 Now the man called his wife's name Eve, because she was the mother of all *the* living.

21 The LORD God made garments of skin for Adam and his wife, and clothed them.

22 Then the LORD God said, "Behold, the man has become like one of Us, knowing good and evil; and now, he might stretch out his hand, and take also from the tree of life, and eat, and live forever"—

23 therefore the LORD God sent him out from the garden of Eden, to cultivate the ground from which he was taken.

24 So He drove the man out; and at the east of the garden of Eden He stationed the cherubim and the flaming sword which turned every direction to guard the way to the tree of life.

Chapter 4

1 Now the man had relations with his wife Eve, and she conceived and gave birth to Cain, and she said, "I have gotten a manchild with *the help of* the LORD."

2 Again, she gave birth to his brother Abel. And Abel was a keeper of flocks, but Cain was a tiller of the ground.

3 So it came about in the course of time that Cain brought an offering to the LORD of the fruit of the ground.

4 Abel, on his part also brought of the firstlings of his flock and of their fat portions. And the LORD had regard for Abel and for his offering;

5 but for Cain and for his offering He had no regard. So Cain became very angry and his countenance fell.

6 Then the LORD said to Cain, "Why are you angry? And why has your countenance fallen?

7 "If you do well, will not *your countenance* be lifted up? And if you do not do well, sin is crouching at the door; and its desire is for you, but you must master it."

8 Cain told Abel his brother. And it came about when they were in the field, that Cain rose up against Abel his brother and killed him.

9 Then the LORD said to Cain, "Where is Abel your brother?" And he said, "I do not know. Am I my brother's keeper?"

10 He said, "What have you done? The voice of your brother's blood is crying to Me from the ground.

11 "Now you are cursed from the ground, which has opened its mouth to receive your brother's blood from your hand.

12 "When you cultivate the ground, it will no longer yield its strength to you; you will be a vagrant and a wanderer on the earth."

13 Cain said to the LORD, "My punishment is too great to bear!

14 "Behold, You have driven me this day from the face of the ground; and from Your face I will be hidden, and I will be a vagrant and a wanderer on the earth, and whoever finds me will kill me."

15 So the LORD said to him, "Therefore whoever kills Cain, vengeance will be taken on him sevenfold." And the LORD appointed a sign for Cain, so that no one finding him would slay him.

16 Then Cain went out from the presence of the LORD, and settled in the land of Nod, east of Eden.

17 Cain had relations with his wife and she conceived, and gave birth to Enoch; and he built a city, and called the name of the city Enoch, after the name of his son.

18 Now to Enoch was born Irad, and Irad became the father of Mehujael, and Mehujael became the father of Methushael, and Methushael became the father of Lamech.

19 Lamech took to himself two wives: the name of the one was Adah, and the name of the other, Zillah.

20 Adah gave birth to Jabal; he was the father of those who dwell in tents and *have* livestock.

21 His brother's name was Jubal; he was the father of all those who play the lyre and pipe.

22 As for Zillah, she also gave birth to Tubal-cain, the forger of all implements of bronze and iron; and the sister of Tubal-cain was Naamah.

23 Lamech said to his wives,

"Adah and Zillah,

Listen to my voice,

You wives of Lamech,

Give heed to my speech,

For I have killed a man for wounding me;

And a boy for striking me;

24 If Cain is avenged sevenfold,

Then Lamech seventy-sevenfold."

25 Adam had relations with his wife again; and she gave birth to a son, and named him Seth, for, *she said,* "God has appointed me another offspring in place of Abel, for Cain killed him."

26 To Seth, to him also a son was born; and he called his name Enosh. Then *men* began to call upon the name of the LORD.

Chapter 5

1 This is the book of the generations of Adam. In the day when God created man, He made him in the likeness of God.

2 He created them male and female, and He blessed them and named them Man in the day when they were created.

3 When Adam had lived one hundred and thirty years, he became the father of *a son* in his own likeness, according to his image, and named him Seth.

4 Then the days of Adam after he became the father of Seth were eight hundred years, and he had *other* sons and daughters.

5 So all the days that Adam lived were nine hundred and thirty years, and he died.

6 Seth lived one hundred and five years, and became the father of Enosh.

7 Then Seth lived eight hundred and seven years after he became the father of Enosh, and he had *other* sons and daughters.

8 So all the days of Seth were nine hundred and twelve years, and he died.

9 Enosh lived ninety years, and became the father of Kenan.

10 Then Enosh lived eight hundred and fifteen years after he became the father of Kenan, and he had *other* sons and daughters.

11 So all the days of Enosh were nine hundred and five years, and he died.

12 Kenan lived seventy years, and became the father of Mahalalel.

13 Then Kenan lived eight hundred and forty years after he became the father of Mahalalel, and he had *other* sons and daughters.

14 So all the days of Kenan were nine hundred and ten years, and he died.

15 Mahalalel lived sixty-five years, and became the father of Jared.

16 Then Mahalalel lived eight hundred and thirty years after he became the father of Jared, and he had *other* sons and daughters.

17 So all the days of Mahalalel were eight hundred and ninety-five years, and he died.

18 Jared lived one hundred and sixty-two years, and became the father of Enoch.

19 Then Jared lived eight hundred years after he became the father of Enoch, and he had *other* sons and daughters.

20 So all the days of Jared were nine hundred and sixty-two years, and he died.

21 Enoch lived sixty-five years, and became the father of Methuselah.

22 Then Enoch walked with God three hundred years after he became the father of Methuselah, and he had *other* sons and daughters.

23 So all the days of Enoch were three hundred and sixty-five years.

24 Enoch walked with God; and he was not, for God took him.

25 Methuselah lived one hundred and eighty-seven years, and became the father of Lamech.

26 Then Methuselah lived seven hundred and eighty-two years after he became the father of Lamech, and he had *other* sons and daughters.

27 So all the days of Methuselah were nine hundred and sixty-nine years, and he died.

28 Lamech lived one hundred and eighty-two years, and became the father of a son.

29 Now he called his name Noah, saying, "This one will give us rest from our work and from the toil of our hands *arising* from the ground which the LORD has cursed."

30 Then Lamech lived five hundred and ninety-five years after he became the father of Noah, and he had *other* sons and daughters.

31 So all the days of Lamech were seven hundred and seventy-seven years, and he died.

32 Noah was five hundred years old, and Noah became the father of Shem, Ham, and Japheth.

Chapter 6

1 Now it came about, when men began to multiply on the face of the land, and daughters were born to them,

2 that the sons of God saw that the daughters of men were beautiful; and they took wives for themselves, whomever they chose.

3 Then the LORD said, "My Spirit shall not strive with man forever, because he also is flesh; nevertheless his days shall be one hundred and twenty years."

4 The Nephilim were on the earth in those days, and also afterward, when the sons of God came in to the daughters of men, and they bore *children* to them. Those were the mighty men who *were* of old, men of renown.

5 Then the LORD saw that the wickedness of man was great on the earth, and that every intent of the thoughts of his heart was only evil continually.

6 The LORD was sorry that He had made man on the earth, and He was grieved in His heart.

7 The LORD said, "I will blot out man whom I have created from the face of the land, from man to animals to creeping things and to birds of the sky; for I am sorry that I have made them."

8 But Noah found favor in the eyes of the LORD.

9 These are *the records of* the generations of Noah. Noah was a righteous man, blameless in his time; Noah walked with God.

10 Noah became the father of three sons: Shem, Ham, and Japheth.

11 Now the earth was corrupt in the sight of God, and the earth was filled with violence.

12 God looked on the earth, and behold, it was corrupt; for all flesh had corrupted their way upon the earth.

13 Then God said to Noah, "The end of all flesh has come before Me; for the earth is filled with violence because of them; and behold, I am about to destroy them with the earth.

14 "Make for yourself an ark of gopher wood; you shall make the ark with rooms, and shall cover it inside and out with pitch.

15 "This is how you shall make it: the length of the ark three hundred cubits, its breadth fifty cubits, and its height thirty cubits.

16 "You shall make a window for the ark, and finish it to a cubit from the top; and set the door of the ark in the side of it; you shall make it with lower, second, and third decks.

17 "Behold, I, even I am bringing the flood of water upon the earth, to destroy all flesh in which is the breath of life, from under heaven; everything that is on the earth shall perish.

18 "But I will establish My covenant with you; and you shall enter the ark—you and your sons and your wife, and your sons' wives with you.

19 "And of every living thing of all flesh, you shall bring two of every *kind* into the ark, to keep *them* alive with you; they shall be male and female.

20 "Of the birds after their kind, and of the animals after their kind, of every creeping thing of the ground after its kind, two of every *kind* will come to you to keep *them* alive.

21 "As for you, take for yourself some of all food which is edible, and gather *it* to yourself; and it shall be for food for you and for them."

22 Thus Noah did; according to all that God had commanded him, so he did.

Chapter 7

1 Then the LORD said to Noah, "Enter the ark, you and all your household, for you *alone* I have seen *to be* righteous before Me in this time.

2 "You shall take with you of every clean animal by sevens, a male and his female; and of the animals that are not clean two, a male and his female;

3 also of the birds of the sky, by sevens, male and female, to keep offspring alive on the face of all the earth.

4 "For after seven more days, I will send rain on the earth forty days and forty nights; and I will blot out from the face of the land every living thing that I have made."

5 Noah did according to all that the LORD had commanded him.

6 Now Noah was six hundred years old when the flood of water came upon the earth.

7 Then Noah and his sons and his wife and his sons' wives with him entered the ark because of the water of the flood.

8 Of clean animals and animals that are not clean and birds and everything that creeps on the ground,

9 there went into the ark to Noah by twos, male and female, as God had commanded Noah.

10 It came about after the seven days, that the water of the flood came upon the earth.

11 In the six hundredth year of Noah's life, in the second month, on the seventeenth day of the month, on the same day all the fountains of the great deep burst open, and the floodgates of the sky were opened.

12 The rain fell upon the earth for forty days and forty nights.

13 On the very same day Noah and Shem and Ham and Japheth, the sons of Noah, and Noah's wife and the three wives of his sons with them, entered the ark,

14 they and every beast after its kind, and all the cattle after their kind, and every creeping thing that creeps on the earth after its kind, and every bird after its kind, all sorts of birds.

15 So they went into the ark to Noah, by twos of all flesh in which was the breath of life.

16 Those that entered, male and female of all flesh, entered as God had commanded him; and the LORD closed *it* behind him.

17 Then the flood came upon the earth for forty days, and the water increased and lifted up the ark, so that it rose above the earth.

18 The water prevailed and increased greatly upon the earth, and the ark floated on the surface of the water.

19 The water prevailed more and more upon the earth, so that all the high mountains everywhere under the heavens were covered.

20 The water prevailed fifteen cubits higher, and the mountains were covered.

21 All flesh that moved on the earth perished, birds and cattle and beasts and every swarming thing that swarms upon the earth, and all mankind;

22 of all that was on the dry land, all in whose nostrils was the breath of the spirit of life, died.

23 Thus He blotted out every living thing that was upon the face of the land, from man to animals to creeping things and to birds of the sky, and they were blotted out from the earth; and only Noah was left, together with those that were with him in the ark.

24 The water prevailed upon the earth one hundred and fifty days.

Chapter 8

1 But God remembered Noah and all the beasts and all the cattle that were with him in the ark; and God caused a wind to pass over the earth, and the water subsided.

2 Also the fountains of the deep and the floodgates of the sky were closed, and the rain from the sky was restrained;

3 and the water receded steadily from the earth, and at the end of one hundred and fifty days the water decreased.

4 In the seventh month, on the seventeenth day of the month, the ark rested upon the mountains of Ararat.

5 The water decreased steadily until the tenth month; in the tenth month, on the first day of the month, the tops of the mountains became visible.

6 Then it came about at the end of forty days, that Noah opened the window of the ark which he had made;

7 and he sent out a raven, and it flew here and there until the water was dried up from the earth.

8 Then he sent out a dove from him, to see if the water was abated from the face of the land;

9 but the dove found no resting place for the sole of her foot, so she returned to him into the ark, for the water was on the surface of

all the earth. Then he put out his hand and took her, and brought her into the ark to himself.

10 So he waited yet another seven days; and again he sent out the dove from the ark.

11 The dove came to him toward evening, and behold, in her beak was a freshly picked olive leaf. So Noah knew that the water was abated from the earth.

12 Then he waited yet another seven days, and sent out the dove; but she did not return to him again.

13 Now it came about in the six hundred and first year, in the first *month,* on the first of the month, the water was dried up from the earth. Then Noah removed the covering of the ark, and looked, and behold, the surface of the ground was dried up.

14 In the second month, on the twenty-seventh day of the month, the earth was dry.

15 Then God spoke to Noah, saying,

16 "Go out of the ark, you and your wife and your sons and your sons' wives with you.

17 "Bring out with you every living thing of all flesh that is with you, birds and animals and every creeping thing that creeps on the earth, that they may breed abundantly on the earth, and be fruitful and multiply on the earth."

18 So Noah went out, and his sons and his wife and his sons' wives with him.

19 Every beast, every creeping thing, and every bird, everything that moves on the earth, went out by their families from the ark.

20 Then Noah built an altar to the LORD, and took of every clean animal and of every clean bird and offered burnt offerings on the altar.

21 The LORD smelled the soothing aroma; and the LORD said to Himself, "I will never again curse the ground on account of man, for the intent of man's heart is evil from his youth; and I will never again destroy every living thing, as I have done.

22 "While the earth remains,
Seedtime and harvest,
And cold and heat,
And summer and winter,
And day and night
Shall not cease."

Chapter 9

1 And God blessed Noah and his sons and said to them, "Be fruitful and multiply, and fill the earth.

2 "The fear of you and the terror of you will be on every beast of the earth and on every bird of the sky; with everything that creeps on the ground, and all the fish of the sea, into your hand they are given.

3 "Every moving thing that is alive shall be food for you; I give all to you, as *I gave* the green plant.

4 "Only you shall not eat flesh with its life, *that is,* its blood.

5 "Surely I will require your lifeblood; from every beast I will require it. And from *every* man, from every man's brother I will require the life of man.

6 "Whoever sheds man's blood,

By man his blood shall be shed,

For in the image of God

He made man.

7 "As for you, be fruitful and multiply;

Populate the earth abundantly and multiply in it."

8 Then God spoke to Noah and to his sons with him, saying,

9 "Now behold, I Myself do establish My covenant with you, and with your descendants after you;

10 and with every living creature that is with you, the birds, the cattle, and every beast of the earth with you; of all that comes out of the ark, even every beast of the earth.

11 "I establish My covenant with you; and all flesh shall never again be cut off by the water of the flood, neither shall there again be a flood to destroy the earth."

12 God said, "This is the sign of the covenant which I am making between Me and you and every living creature that is with you, for all successive generations;

13 I set My bow in the cloud, and it shall be for a sign of a covenant between Me and the earth.

14 "It shall come about, when I bring a cloud over the earth, that the bow will be seen in the cloud,

15 and I will remember My covenant, which is between Me and you and every living creature of all flesh; and never again shall the water become a flood to destroy all flesh.

16 "When the bow is in the cloud, then I will look upon it, to remember the everlasting covenant between God and every living creature of all flesh that is on the earth."

17 And God said to Noah, "This is the sign of the covenant which I have established between Me and all flesh that is on the earth."

18 Now the sons of Noah who came out of the ark were Shem and Ham and Japheth; and Ham was the father of Canaan.

19 These three *were* the sons of Noah, and from these the whole earth was populated.

20 Then Noah began farming and planted a vineyard.

21 He drank of the wine and became drunk, and uncovered himself inside his tent.

22 Ham, the father of Canaan, saw the nakedness of his father, and told his two brothers outside.

23 But Shem and Japheth took a garment and laid it upon both their shoulders and walked backward and covered the nakedness of their father; and their faces were turned away, so that they did not see their father's nakedness.

24 When Noah awoke from his wine, he knew what his youngest son had done to him.

25 So he said,

"Cursed be Canaan;

A servant of servants

He shall be to his brothers."

26 He also said,

"Blessed be the LORD,

The God of Shem;

And let Canaan be his servant.

27 "May God enlarge Japheth,

And let him dwell in the tents of Shem;

And let Canaan be his servant."

28 Noah lived three hundred and fifty years after the flood.

29 So all the days of Noah were nine hundred and fifty years, and he died.

Chapter 10

1 Now these are *the records of* the generations of Shem, Ham, and Japheth, the sons of Noah; and sons were born to them after the flood.

2 The sons of Japheth *were* Gomer and Magog and Madai and Javan and Tubal and Meshech and Tiras.

3 The sons of Gomer *were* Ashkenaz and Riphath and Togarmah.

4 The sons of Javan *were* Elishah and Tarshish, Kittim and Dodanim.

5 From these the coastlands of the nations were separated into their lands, every one according to his language, according to their families, into their nations.

6 The sons of Ham *were* Cush and Mizraim and Put and Canaan.

7 The sons of Cush *were* Seba and Havilah and Sabtah and Raamah and Sabteca; and the sons of Raamah *were* Sheba and Dedan.

8 Now Cush became the father of Nimrod; he became a mighty one on the earth.

9 He was a mighty hunter before the LORD; therefore it is said, "Like Nimrod a mighty hunter before the LORD."

10 The beginning of his kingdom was Babel and Erech and Accad and Calneh, in the land of Shinar.

11 From that land he went forth into Assyria, and built Nineveh and Rehoboth-Ir and Calah,

12 and Resen between Nineveh and Calah; that is the great city.

13 Mizraim became the father of Ludim and Anamim and Lehabim and Naphtuhim

14 and Pathrusim and Casluhim (from which came the Philistines) and Caphtorim.

15 Canaan became the father of Sidon, his firstborn, and Heth

16 and the Jebusite and the Amorite and the Girgashite

17 and the Hivite and the Arkite and the Sinite

18 and the Arvadite and the Zemarite and the Hamathite; and afterward the families of the Canaanite were spread abroad.

19 The territory of the Canaanite extended from Sidon as you go toward Gerar, as far as Gaza; as you go toward Sodom and Gomorrah and Admah and Zeboiim, as far as Lasha.

20 These are the sons of Ham, according to their families, according to their languages, by their lands, by their nations.

21 Also to Shem, the father of all the children of Eber, *and* the older brother of Japheth, children were born.

22 The sons of Shem *were* Elam and Asshur and Arpachshad and Lud and Aram.

23 The sons of Aram *were* Uz and Hul and Gether and Mash.

24 Arpachshad became the father of Shelah; and Shelah became the father of Eber.

25 Two sons were born to Eber; the name of the one *was* Peleg, for in his days the earth was divided; and his brother's name *was* Joktan.

26 Joktan became the father of Almodad and Sheleph and Hazarmaveth and Jerah

27 and Hadoram and Uzal and Diklah

28 and Obal and Abimael and Sheba

29 and Ophir and Havilah and Jobab; all these were the sons of Joktan.

30 Now their settlement extended from Mesha as you go toward Sephar, the hill country of the east.

31 These are the sons of Shem, according to their families, according to their languages, by their lands, according to their nations.

32 These are the families of the sons of Noah, according to their genealogies, by their nations; and out of these the nations were separated on the earth after the flood.

Chapter 11

1 Now the whole earth used the same language and the same words.

2 It came about as they journeyed east, that they found a plain in the land of Shinar and settled there.

3 They said to one another, "Come, let us make bricks and burn *them* thoroughly." And they used brick for stone, and they used tar for mortar.

4 They said, "Come, let us build for ourselves a city, and a tower whose top *will reach* into heaven, and let us make for ourselves a name, otherwise we will be scattered abroad over the face of the whole earth."

5 The LORD came down to see the city and the tower which the sons of men had built.

6 The LORD said, "Behold, they are one people, and they all have the same language. And this is what they began to do, and now nothing which they purpose to do will be impossible for them.

7 "Come, let Us go down and there confuse their language, so that they will not understand one another's speech."

8 So the LORD scattered them abroad from there over the face of the whole earth; and they stopped building the city.

9 Therefore its name was called Babel, because there the LORD confused the language of the whole earth; and from there the LORD scattered them abroad over the face of the whole earth.

10 These are *the records of* the generations of Shem. Shem was one hundred years old, and became the father of Arpachshad two years after the flood;

11 and Shem lived five hundred years after he became the father of Arpachshad, and he had *other* sons and daughters.

12 Arpachshad lived thirty-five years, and became the father of Shelah;

13 and Arpachshad lived four hundred and three years after he became the father of Shelah, and he had *other* sons and daughters.

14 Shelah lived thirty years, and became the father of Eber;

15 and Shelah lived four hundred and three years after he became the father of Eber, and he had *other* sons and daughters.

16 Eber lived thirty-four years, and became the father of Peleg;

17 and Eber lived four hundred and thirty years after he became the father of Peleg, and he had *other* sons and daughters.

18 Peleg lived thirty years, and became the father of Reu;

19 and Peleg lived two hundred and nine years after he became the father of Reu, and he had *other* sons and daughters.

20 Reu lived thirty-two years, and became the father of Serug;

21 and Reu lived two hundred and seven years after he became the father of Serug, and he had *other* sons and daughters.

22 Serug lived thirty years, and became the father of Nahor;

23 and Serug lived two hundred years after he became the father of Nahor, and he had *other* sons and daughters.

24 Nahor lived twenty-nine years, and became the father of Terah;

25 and Nahor lived one hundred and nineteen years after he became the father of Terah, and he had *other* sons and daughters.

26 Terah lived seventy years, and became the father of Abram, Nahor and Haran.

27 Now these are *the records of* the generations of Terah. Terah became the father of Abram, Nahor and Haran; and Haran became the father of Lot.

28 Haran died in the presence of his father Terah in the land of his birth, in Ur of the Chaldeans.

29 Abram and Nahor took wives for themselves. The name of Abram's wife was Sarai; and the name of Nahor's wife was Milcah, the daughter of Haran, the father of Milcah and Iscah.

30 Sarai was barren; she had no child.

31 Terah took Abram his son, and Lot the son of Haran, his grandson, and Sarai his daughter-in-law, his son Abram's wife; and they went out together from Ur of the Chaldeans in order to enter the land of Canaan; and they went as far as Haran, and settled there.

32 The days of Terah were two hundred and five years; and Terah died in Haran.

MORE DISCOVER 4 YOURSELF!® INDUCTIVE BIBLE STUDIES FOR KIDS

Kay Arthur and Cyndy Shearer

Kids "make" a movie to discover who Jesus is and His impact on their lives. Activities and 15-minute lessons make this study of John 1–10 great for all ages!

ISBN 0-7369-0119-1

Kay Arthur, Janna Arndt, Lisa Guest, and Cyndy Shearer

This book picks up where *Jesus in the Spotlight* leaves off: John 11–16. Kids join a movie team to bring the life of Jesus to the big screen in order to learn key truths about prayer, heaven, and Jesus.

ISBN 0-7369-0144-2

Kay Arthur and Janna Arndt

As "advice columnists," kids delve into the book of James to discover—and learn how to apply—the best answers for a variety of problems.

ISBN 0-7369-0148-5

Kay Arthur and Janna Arndt

This easy-to-use Bible study combines serious commitment to God's Word with illustrations and activities that reinforce biblical truth.

ISBN 0-7369-0362-3

Kay Arthur and Janna Arndt

Focusing on John 17–21, children become "directors" who must discover the details of Jesus' life to make a great movie. They also learn how to get the most out of reading their Bibles.

ISBN 0-7369-0546-4

Kay Arthur and Scoti Domeij

As "reporters," kids investigate Jonah's story and conduct interviews. Using puzzles and activities, these lessons highlight God's loving care and the importance of obedience.

ISBN 0-7369-0203-1

Kay Arthur and Janna Arndt

Kids become archaeologists to uncover how God deals with sin, where different languages and nations came from, and what God's plan is for saving people (Genesis 3–11).

ISBN 0-7369-0374-7

Kay Arthur and Janna Arndt

God's Amazing Creation covers Genesis 1–2—those awesome days when God created the stars, the world, the sea, the animals, and the very first people. Young explorers will go on an archaeological dig to discover truths for themselves!

ISBN 0-7369-0143-4

Kay Arthur and Janna Arndt

The Lord's Prayer is the foundation of this special basic training, and it's not long before the trainees discover the awesome truth that God wants to talk to them as much as they want to talk to Him!

ISBN 0-7369-0666-5

Kay Arthur and Janna Arndt

Readers head out on the rugged Oregon Trail to discover the lessons Abraham learned when he left his home and moved to an unknown land. Kids will face the excitement, fears, and blessings of faith.

ISBN 0-7369-0936-2

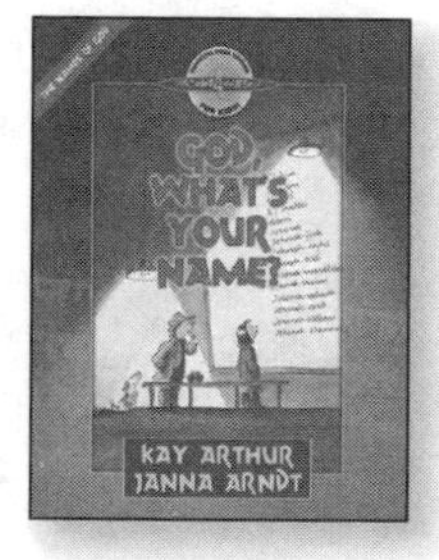

Kay Arthur and Janna Arndt

This exciting book leads the reader on a journey to God's heart using the inductive study method and the wonder of an adventurous spy tale.

ISBN 0-7369-1161-8

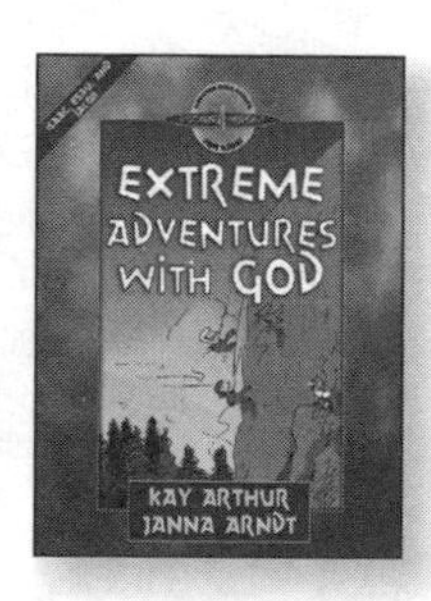

Kay Arthur and Janna Arndt

This engaging, high-energy addition to the Discover 4 Yourself series examines the journeys of Isaac, Jacob, and Esau and reveals how God outfits His children with everything they need for life's difficulties, victories, and extreme adventures.

ISBN 0-7369-0937-0

Kay Arthur and Janna Arndt

This exciting addition invites children to solve great mysteries about the future using the inductive study method and the power of a fun story.

ISBN 0-7369-1527-3